RELENTLESS

RELENTLESS

THE STORY OF DAX CRUM AS TOLD BY
HIS FATHER RICHARD CRUM

BONNEVILLE BOOKS
SPRINGVILLE, UTAH

Some photographs courtesy of Garrett Davis, *Spectrum and Daily News,* Cedar City, UT, and *The Daily Times*, Farmington, NM.

ISBN 13: 978-1-59955-464-8

Published by Bonneville Books, an imprint of Cedar Fort, Inc.,
2373 W. 700 S., Springville, UT 84663
Distributed by Cedar Fort, Inc., www.cedarfort.com

LIBRARY OF CONGRESS CATALOGING-IN-PUBLICATION DATA
Crum, Richard D., 1954-
  Relentless / Richard D. Crum and Dax Crum.
    p. cm.
  Summary: The story of Dax Crum, a boy who excels in sports in spite of missing one hand.
  ISBN 978-1-59955-464-8
  1. Crum, Dax, 1984- 2. Athletes--Biography. I. Crum, Dax, 1984- II. Title.
  GV697.C78C78 2010
  796.092--dc22
  [B]
                          2010033001

Cover design by Danie Romrell
Cover design © 2011 by Lyle Mortimer
Edited and typeset by Melissa J. Caldwell

Printed in the United States of America

10 9 8 7 6 5 4 3 2 1

Printed on acid-free paper

To my beautiful wife and Dax's mother,
our greatest fan.

CONTENTS

Contents

Dax sits in the middle of his two cousins, using his stub to steady himself.

As a candidate for a toe to stub transplant, Dax poses for a hand photo for the Shriner's Hospital in Los Angeles.

Older sister Vanessa and Dax. Often, Vanessa had to "mind" Dax, but if she tried to manually lead him, he demanded she hold his stub. In her early teens, Vanessa's basketball skills inspired Dax to practice harder.

Dax, wearing the "crash helmet," poses with his brother Justin.

Dax performs the careful act of one-handed shoe tying.

At the grandparents' insistence, Dax repeats the skill. This time the grandmothers would not have their "baby" sitting on the floor.

Dax practiced everywhere he could from indoor gyms to outside courts, even in Los Angeles, CA.

Dax, with brother Baric, learned a lot growing up on a farm. He would often help his brothers feed the pigs.

Dax, age 9, learned to be a team player by participating in youth sports. He loved to steal bases in baseball.

19-KIRTLAND-93

Dax (#15) played a variety of sports, including football, soccer, baseball, and basketball.

Dax, top row, third from right.

Preface

I WOULD LIKE TO THANK THE MANY PEOPLE WHO HAVE assisted my son Dax over the past twenty-plus years of his life, especially the coaches who took a chance by putting him on the floor, field, or court. I want to thank those who were his opponents and persevered under oppressing defense but lived through it.

I wondered for several years whether I should undertake this bold step of writing a book for others to step into Dax's life. Numerous people have inquired into his abilities and challenges: How does he do it? How does he manage? Considering these questions, I wondered who would be interested in reading this book. Should it be written for youth or adults? Should it be a self-help book or a narrative? Who would benefit from these words? It finally came to me when I watched Dax play in Southern Utah.

This book is dedicated to the man in Texas who is adjusting to life because he lost his hand in a farm accident. He called after Dax won his first state championship in basketball and wanted to know how Dax manages to be so normal in everyday activities.

It is written for the one-handed girl in Nevada who heard of Dax from a national magazine, was amazed to learn that he was a starter on a high school basketball team, and called to introduce herself.

It is written for the family in Idaho who loaded up the car and drove for seven hours to Southern Utah to take Dax out to dinner. They interviewed him for four hours so that their children could see and learn "first hand" how he thinks and operates in a two-handed world.

This book is written for the little boy in Albuquerque, New Mexico, who bravely walked out onto the floor at the end of the playoff game and tugged on Dax's jersey so he could talk to his hero.

It is written for the mother in Wisconsin who drove her one-handed son to Illinois to watch Dax play and meet him in person after a Division I basketball game.

It is written for the woman who is troubled by the cloudy sonogram of her unborn baby.

It is written for the woman who just gave birth to a mal-formed baby and is considering a lawsuit against her doctor because of the betrayal and trauma she feels.

This book is written for the people who have seen a one-handed person accomplishing things that are difficult in their two-handed world.

It is written to aspiring, reluctant, and intimidated athletes who have just entered college and want to walk onto the college team.

It is written for the many young people who have struggled to be part of a group or team and have given sweat and tears just to fit in.

It is written for those of us who watch Dax in amazement as he performs feats of athleticism that we only wish we could accomplish.

This book is written for all those people who watched Dax play and never knew he was one handed until somebody pointed it out.

This book is written for all the fans in the stands who pointed to the one-handed boy and sat with tear-filled eyes.

This book is written for two great family patriarchs who could not wait to watch their grandson master the new sport but died before seeing him reach his ultimate goal.

This book is written to Dax's mother, who fiercely defended her son from countless referees who did not recognize the one-handed backspin dribble and consequently called "traveling" on her boy.

This book is written and published because I have felt a tremendous need to repay the kindnesses and tender mercies that have been shown to us by so many. Dave Thomas, the founder of Wendy's, said, "Share your success and help others succeed. Give everyone a piece of the pie. If the pie's not big enough, make a bigger pie."[1]

Sharing this "pie" will be sharing our success. Several struggle with so many problems, and I hope this book touches their lives and helps them to find the determination for success.

INTRODUCTION

Eight seconds were left in the game, and Kirtland Central High School was behind by one point. Reserve, a small town in central New Mexico, had the ball and were prepared to stall for the win. Kirtland Central had never been to a state championship basketball game, and this was my chance to win and be a hero.

Reserve's point guard brought the ball down the right side of the court and made a backspin dribble to move across the court, but just then I saw an opening to steal the ball and go for the winning layup. I knew I could beat the opposition to the basket and win the game for the team. I stole the ball, and adrenaline carried me to the basket. The crowd stood in preparation for the championship celebration as I glided in and placed the ball on the painted square. But it was too high, and the ball ricocheted back to the free throw line, where the trailing opponent picked it up. I fouled him, and he shot two free throws to increase their margin of victory. If you drive to Reserve, New Mexico, today, you will see a greeting sign that states: "Reserve 1972 State Champions Basketball, 2A Division."

* * *

I had many challenges in my life, including the death of my father when I was five years old. I missed him deeply. The entire community attended his viewing at my house. Two aunts tried to console me that evening, but when they reached over to hug me, I refused, something I regret to this day. Even then, I wished I had let them hug me, but I felt a lot of self-pity and anger. My father was not going to be around. Mom said that I was just lonely, but she realized that I was more than she could handle and I needed help. She would not let one of her children fail in life due to hardship.

My mom lost her smile. Many times I saw her turn and look at me as I sat in front of our small television. I now know what she was thinking: *What am I going to do with this troubled son? I cannot allow him to sorrow any longer. Where should I take him? Can I get someone else to help me raise him? Do I dare give him up to someone else to raise? I hate having to ask somebody for help, but I might have to swallow even more of my pride.*

After a long, boring summer, school was about to start, and Mom knew she had to act. There was no kindergarten, and barely enough kids to even have a school. It didn't matter. Mom wanted me in school, and she told the principal that I was going to be in school that year even though I was too young. Her compassion matched her passion, and I was quickly allowed to be a first grader.

Mom was also grateful for those who recognized her need. I was two days late for the start of class, but Mom and the principal had secretly arranged with the first grade teacher to have a little party to welcome me into the class. The teacher had all of the kids bring their favorite toys from home, and I was allowed to use them all for about ten minutes. I smiled, and then I saw Mom smile.

But she wasn't done yet. When I got out of school, she

met me before I got on the bus. She told me that I was going to go to Uncle Erwin's house to help chop cotton, which meant walking up and down rows of cotton fields and eliminating the weeds from around the cotton plants. Cotton hates competition. About the time you get done with "chopping," it is time to pick it. I was too little to pull one of the big bags, so I walked beside my big cousins and put it in their bags.

My uncle Erwin was very athletic, hard working, and hard playing. He was great with five-year-old children. A man of integrity, he was determined to get things done and didn't allow his children to be lazy. When we finished in the fields, however, it was time to play basketball or kick the can. He always said, "A change is as good as a rest." Mom knew Uncle Erwin was the kind of man that I should emulate.

Through good examples and loving people, I overcame my hurt, anger, and other challenges. I would have never gotten to that championship game without their encouragement and support.

* * *

Almost thirty years later, my third-born son was struggling to be a champion. Newspapers and magazines questioned his ability to play. Was he even a legitimate player? I was a senior when I played in my championship game, but he was just a sophomore. Perennial 4A powerhouse Albuquerque Academy was supposed to win. Knock down these free throws, and he could seal the victory for Kirtland. The radio announcer said, "After what this kid has been through, these are going in! This kid is ice."

This moment could spell success or defeat for him. His goal to become a Division I basketball player was on the line. Adrenaline again surged. The crowd stood in anticipation. A championship was close.

Miss, and lose.

Deliver, and win.

But there was something special about this drama—this "kid" only had one hand.

Chapter 1

EXPECT THE UNEXPECTED

Valerie was expecting, but no sonograms were taken. The doctors at the Regional Medical Center were usually late and this, our fourth time, was no exception. In her struggle, beads of sweat turned into little streams, and I wiped them like a dutiful husband. With every painful contraction, Valerie squeezed the tips of my fingers until they turned purple. A lady two rooms down the hall was telling her wonderful husband what he was made of, but I never heard him respond.

Occasionally, Valerie would make a small, almost imperceptible groan. She knew exactly what to expect. The doctor came into the room just when Valerie was about to lose her patience, and he and I reached to catch the baby at the same time. I imagined what would be said of me if the baby hit the floor, suffered brain damage, and was labeled handicapped all its life. The nurse standing in the corner didn't lift a finger until the doctor told her it was a healthy boy. I smiled and looked back at Valerie, and she asked, "Is he okay?" She let go of my fingers, and I went to check for her.

The nurse wiped the baby down, letting the heat lamp keep him warm. He was lying on his right side. I looked up and down the baby and noticed he had all ten toes. I winked at Valerie, and she was relieved. Inspecting the baby was the father's job, and I had to do it right.

SIDE BY SIDE WITH GRIEF LIES JOY.

Fran Drescher

I looked at the baby's left hand that was waving at me, and it had all its fingers. When I looked for the right hand, it was inside the baby's mouth. Yes, the entire hand was in the baby's mouth. I instinctively reached to get the hand out of the baby's mouth, but the nurse stopped me and told me it was okay. I didn't want my child to be a thumb sucker, and already he was sucking on his *entire* hand.

Then the nurse turned the baby, and there it was—or rather, there it wasn't. There was no hand. Instead of a right hand there was only a stub and a mini-thumb much shorter than a normal thumb. The baby wasn't sucking his whole hand; he had no hand to suck on. It looked like it had started to grow at one time but then just gave up. Valerie asked me if the baby was all right. She must have sensed that I was not acting normally. I didn't know what to say. I took a couple of steps back, turned to Valerie, and said, "He doesn't have a right hand."

I wished I hadn't said it. Valerie turned her head into her right shoulder, away from all of us. It was important to her to give birth to a healthy baby. I knew she felt that I would not be proud of the child. I still didn't know what to say. I did the dad thing and paced back and forth several times, but the stub never changed.

The nurse wrapped him up and took him over to Valerie, and she cuddled him. It was the quickest case of grieving I have ever witnessed in my life. She immediately looked up at me to get approval. I smiled a worried smile at her, and I could tell she felt the same. Is this baby normal? Is the baby just minus a hand or does it go further? Valerie immediately became protective of this little boy.

My heart was stretched so that new, protective, caring muscles grew inside. My other children say that Dax is my favorite, but it really isn't a matter of favoritism. This little guy required new parenting skills, and Valerie and I immediately expanded our own thinking upon seeing Dax. It took more time, energy, and patience. Neither of us wanted our baby to be "challenged." I quickly questioned my ability to raise a boy who only had one hand.

Then, the doctor did something that would be repeated many times throughout the next twenty years of Dax's life. When the doctor initially handed the baby to the nurse, he completely overlooked that the baby was one handed. When he inspected the baby, he then noticed the right stub. He asked, "How did I miss that?" He checked the baby's chest and arm muscles, looked up at me, and said, "He's going to be just fine." Valerie and I leaned our heads together, probably to show each other that we were good with what we had, but to be honest we weren't sure. One thing we did know though: we didn't want the other to be disappointed.

When I brought the older kids to the hospital to see the new baby, I took off the mitten from Dax's right arm. Justin said, "Whoa, Dad, that's weird!" His other brother, Baric, became protective and later told his cousins that his little brother was just as good as their little brothers. When four-year-old Vanessa looked at him for the first time, she was shocked and tearfully exclaimed, "Why did they cut off his fingers?"

> **WISDOM IS LEARNING WHAT TO OVERLOOK.**
>
> *William James*

When we took Dax home, we had an interesting dilemma. Valerie did not nurse any of her children. Each baby learned to hold a bottle and followed the same eating routine. With Dax, we propped the bottle up with a pillow, not even trying to have him hold it, but instinctively he would reach for it. Within a few months, he wanted to hold the bottle himself when he drank. Besides using his stub as a pacifier, this was his first task to learn how to manipulate an object. One meaning for the first three letters of the word *manipulate* is "hand." How can a baby manipulate an object if there is no hand?

Dax put his tiny thumblike finger on the top of the bottle, but the bottle fell off on his right side. Over and over he would put his short right thumb on the top of the bottle, and he would lose it. I turned his hand around so that the stub thumb would support the bottle from the bottom. He never did it my way. Eventually, he simply applied more pressure and pushed the bottle into the other hand with more force. I didn't realize how many times this learning scenario would be repeated with Dax. I would show him a way to do something, and then he would show me how it should be done the one-handed way.

Deal with the Hand You're Dealt

This boy was going to be different, but how should we raise him? Parents with special children know what I mean. It seemed that with every venture in his childhood, people told us to "just go ahead and accept him for what he is." Numerous times I heard, "Your son is handicapped. Just accept it."

We heard it when we decided to take Dax to Los Angeles and see if they could "give him a finger." The surgical procedure would take Dax's second toe and put it on his stump, allowing him to clamp or even grasp if the transplant was long enough to reach the short thumb. Valerie talked with the Shriners at the hospital, and they paid for the trip. She returned and told me about the procedure, and I asked her if she thought it could work. She didn't know. The second time back from Los Angeles, she told me that she couldn't decide. She didn't want to make the decision to cut off one of her baby's toes. The thought of harming her baby was appalling. I thought, "It takes a man to make this kind of decision."

The third time, I flew to LA and had a great visit with a Japanese doctor who was very cordial, interesting, and knowledgeable. He told me that the procedure to remove a toe and transplant it to Dax's hand needed to be done as soon as possible because the younger the child is, the more likely the toe would not be rejected from the hand. Rejection was far more likely in the 1980s than it is now. It was a risky procedure.

The doctor then asked if I had seen what God had given Dax. I asked him to clarify with an, "Excuse me?" He explained, "When God takes away, he gives something in return. Have you seen what it is that God has given him?" I said, "Yes," even though I really hadn't thought about it. Did Dax have superhuman hearing, strength, or heat vision? I wanted something amazing to make up for what was taken from him.

SEE WHAT THE LORD HATH DONE

On the way home, I wondered what it was that I would tell Valerie and the family. Could I allow somebody to cut off one of my son's toes? What if the toe was rejected by his stub? What would people think of me as the father of a 6½-fingered, 9-toed son? Is this better than a 10-toed, 5½-fingered son? I kept thinking of what others might say: "Shame on you for letting them do that to your son." When I arrived home, Valerie asked me if I had made my decision, but I couldn't answer her. I wanted to talk with my mom and dad, who advised me to pray about it. I did and realized that I couldn't allow the procedure.

DIFFERENCES CHALLENGE ASSUMPTIONS.

Anne Wilson Schaef

When I discussed it with others, they would say, "We're okay with him." What they really were saying was, "Why can't you accept what God made?" I was fine with what God had made. I was just troubled with what he hadn't made. Why couldn't I just accept it? The very phrase seemed to shout, "Give up!" and that was something I could never accept because I was born into a family of competitors.

My mother, Elaine Richardson, was swift on her feet, and according to witnesses, my father had been very coordinated. I myself was an all-state defensive back in high school football, and I also set my high school pole vault record at 13½ feet at the state decathlon. I was a humbled basketball player. Dax's grandfather was an excellent distance runner. Dax's uncle played college basketball in Nevada. I knew my children would learn how to compete. Giving up meant I was not able to to raise my son to be a competitor. Competing was in our blood. Giving up was for others, but not for me. Valerie and I would never give up on teaching him what God had given him.

Chapter 2

CREATIVE PROBLEM SOLVING

As a toddler, Dax was extremely active. He liked to try everything. By today's standards, he had the most inflamed case of ADHD (Attention Deficit Hyperactive Disorder) that you have ever seen. Running, jumping, and causing trouble were second-nature activities. When we fall, it's natural for us to put out two hands and catch ourselves. When Dax fell, however, he would land on his left hand and right stub, his body would rotate to the right, and the right side of his face would hit the ground first. It happened so many times—he falls, face hits the ground, blood spurts from cuts, swelling starts, he comes up crying, we comfort him and wipe off blood, he runs off, and we worry about what the relatives will think. We often picked the pebbles out from underneath the skin or iced down massive goose eggs. Next thing we knew, Dax was running right into the next pole, door, or pit.

We solved this problem by getting him a bicycle helmet, nicknaming it the "crash helmet." Dax wore the crash helmet for the next few months, especially when he went outdoors. He didn't like it, but we didn't want him to have brain damage. At extended family get-togethers, the family thought it was an ingenious idea, especially the mothers who had great concern for him.

MOTHER'S WATCH

We had a small hog farm that the "big boys" worked while I did shift work at a New Mexico power plant. Valerie was home with Dax for the day until his two brothers, Baric and Justin, and his sister, Vanessa, returned from school. The little one-handed rascal would run out to greet the school bus, many times wearing nothing but his Spiderman "undies." He loved his siblings, especially his brothers. He worshipped them. They were bigger, cooler, and stronger. He wanted to do everything they were doing. You'd always hear him begging, "Can I come? Please!"

Valerie attempted naps to alleviate Dax's stimulation and helmet time, but they seemed to always happen just as the big boys were getting home. They would often begin their chores while Dax was supposed to be asleep. Welding gates, feeding hogs, and harvesting the corn were manly jobs, and Dax wanted hand(s)-on experience. Once, after contemplating his escape, he popped out of bed and made his way to his bedroom window. Moving the furniture to get him at eye level, he kicked the window screen out. Turning around backward, he lowered himself down, scraping his belly on the metal frame until his feet hit the ground.

> PARENTS CAN REALLY HELP, BUT THEY CAN ALSO REALLY HINDER.
>
> *Mike Krzyzewski*

Dax made his way through the pasture to the pigpens to help his brothers. The work was soon done, and the Crum boys started walking toward the house for dinner and homework. Valerie, while washing dishes, looked out the window to the field and saw the third Crum not in the place she had left him. Their eyes met, and Dax knew he was caught, but the child in him thought that if he could make it back to his bed, the wrath of Mom would pass him by. He sprinted around the house back to his window. With a running start, his one hand barely caught hold of the window ledge. He made it back to bed safe and sound, just as Valerie opened the door. He sat up stretching and yawning, and said, "Oh! Hello, Mother."

Valerie escorted him to the bathtub by his ear to scrub off the pig smell. She barely controlled her laughter, loving his ingenuity and enthusiasm. She knew it would take a careful watch and much more discipline to mold that tenacity. We were now starting to see what God had given him. His will, determination, and intellect were his gifts from God—they were his superpowers. From then on, naps were taken on a blanket where mother could keep a close watch.

No Fear

Like Valerie, I also learned that Dax needed closer attention but in a more dangerous setting. My eldest son, Baric, was competing in the javelin at the New Mexico state track meet. The year before, he had won the event with a throw of 180 feet. The javelin field was south of the regular stadium, and we were allowed to stand among the trees that surround the area. Nobody was allowed out in the javelin landing area for obvious reasons.

As I and my other children watched the event, I held Dax's little arm. Every time Baric let go of a toss, Dax would mimic his movements. Baric's throws were not as good as the year before, and Dax was trying to help his champion brother with each throw. He was a great supporter. I held onto Dax so he would not get in the throwing field. On Baric's last throw, the javelin sailed out to about two hundred feet. We all spontaneously started clapping. I couldn't hear Dax's clapping because his one-handed claps just weren't that loud. Before I knew it, Dax was at the two hundred–foot line, pulling his big brother's javelin out of the ground and running it back to the scratch line. Fortunately, it was also the last throw of the contest, so no more javelins were scheduled for launch. We got lucky—lucky Valerie didn't see and lucky all that happened was the field judges harshly and vehemently cautioning us on safety boundaries. I knew that Dax's competitive spirit was alive and well.

Chapter 3

No "Special" Privileges

D ax had to make adjustments in things that two-handed people never give a second thought. It is quite simple to eat a bowl of cereal with one hand. One bowl of cereal and one mouth—no problem. But can a growing boy continue to eat just cereal every day? What happens when it's a pork chop on the plate? Should we insist that he cut his meat or should we cut it for him the rest of his childhood? Do we pray that he'll marry someone who will cut his meat for him when they go out for the evening to a fancy restaurant? Should we just let him pick it up by the bone and chew pieces off bit by bit? Should we indeed cap his hand with a prosthetic pinching device? Should we raise him normally or try to get him as many "special" privileges as possible? What's normal?

By the time Dax was four years old, Valerie and I knew we needed to make solid decisions on how we would raise this "handicapped" son.

TIE 'EM UP TIGHT

Every day Dax's motor skills improved. As I watched him accomplish task after task, I simply made the decision that Dax needed to be "normal." I didn't want him to be treated as "handicapped." One day, I stopped using the "H" word altogether; in fact, our family never used the word after I decided that. He was expected to accomplish everything our other children were expected to accomplish, and he was going to be a hard worker—do his daily chores and study his scriptures and his textbooks. He was expected to look and act like a Crum right down to the appropriate clothes.

One day as he strapped up his Velcro shoes to go play, I knelt in front of him. I told him that he would not be allowed to go to school until he learned to tie his shoes. He still had one year to go, but our other kids learned before they went to school. Surprised, I saw some fear in his eyes for the first time, and he realized that there weren't going to be any excuses. I told him, "You cannot expect your teachers to tie your shoes just because you only have one hand." He was really looking forward to school and the other kids, so he replied, "All right."

From behind me, a stern voice said, "Dax Mitchell Crum! What do you say?" Valerie used his middle name to emphasize the significance and the seriousness of his answer.

"Yes, sir," Dax responded softly.

We went into the living room and sat face-to-face. I set a new shoe box on the ground between us. He pulled his new canvas sneakers out of the box, examining them for coolness. He liked them a lot, and I think that set his determination on fire. Over the next few hours, I showed him how shoes could be tied in a bow. I moved slowly and walked him through the steps. The rabbit came out of the hole, went around the tree, and hopped back down the hole. Then, if he had done it correctly, the pull of a shoelace would make the knot disappear. He took over working the laces. I jumped in frequently and showed him correct string positions.

Finally, in frustration Dax snapped at me, "Dad, you are messing me up. Let me do it." I was trying to show him the two-handed way to tie shoes. I stepped back and realized I couldn't do it for him. The struggle was his. It was a hard lesson Dax taught me that day: sometimes you must let your kids struggle. He was up to it. Like a lion cub, he was ready to hunt.

THE SHOW IS ALWAYS SO MUCH FUN.

Kurt Browning

He was done hearing about rabbits and loops, swoops, and pulls. His tongue went to work as hard as his hand(s). Hours went by. I peeked in periodically from around the corner, until the hunt was over.

"Dad," he called long and braggingly. I watched the short thumb on his right hand serve as the loop maker, like a crochet hook, as he twisted and pulled. Then his two little thumbs stretched out his bow. "Ta-da!" Next came the finale, the test. He pulled one of the strings. The bow disappeared. Perfect. We promised Dax that when he had practiced enough, we would call his grandparents so he could show them his new skill.

The day finally arrived. Grandfather Marion walked over from their house next door and asked what we needed. I said that we had something to show him as soon as Grandpa Merwyn arrived from Kirtland—ten miles away.

With four grandparents in the room, I asked both grandfathers to take a seat in the middle of the floor. There was just enough room between them for Dax to sit. I told him to come into the living room and show them what he had learned. He walked in with one shoe untied. These patriarchs knew what was coming, and they moved in closer. I quietly said, "Dax has something to show you." He sat down between them and slowly started to work the strings. He had to carefully lay them across each other. Then he stuck out his tongue, and he gave it all he had. What had taken him hours to master was now performed in just a miracle-filled minute, but it was just enough time for both grandpas to sniffle.

A HERO IS AN ORDINARY INDI-
VIDUAL WHO FINDS STRENGTH
TO PERSEVERE AND ENDURE
IN SPITE OF OVERWHELMING
OBSTACLES.

Christopher Reeve

Grandfather Marion hugged him first and said, "Atta boy!" Grandpa Merwyn, the WWII veteran, put both arms around him, kissed him on the cheek, and said, "You're my hero." We all started to cry. This was what Dax needed. He needed approval. He needed men who were in authority to say, "You're going to be okay."

Grandmother Norma scooped him in and gave him a huge hug, leaving a little mascara on both of his cheeks. Grandma Elaine, my mother, said, "He can do anything he wants." Then she hugged him. My heart swelled bigger than any of theirs. Dax had a troubled look on his face because of all the tears, but I assured him that they were all happy tears.

I have wondered about what Grandpa Merwyn said for several years now. He used a powerful word for something that seemed to be such a simple act. Here was a man who had numerous people to consider heroic. He had fought in World War II and had seen men die for their country. Yet Dax was his hero. Edgar Watson Howe's definition of a hero helped me to understand better: "A boy doesn't have to go to war to be a hero; he can say he doesn't like pie when he sees there isn't enough to go around."

Chapter 4

FIRST GRADE CHALLENGES

Dax started the first grade, and it wasn't long before we got a call to please come directly to the school and have a conference with the school counselor. Dax's first grade teacher was having a "real" problem with him in class. I went to the school, and the counselor wouldn't describe the problem to me but sent me to talk to the teacher. My imagination ran wild because I knew how energetic and aggressive Dax could be. Had he hurt another student? Was he rude to his teacher? Had he been mean to another student on the playground?

His classroom, of course, was the last one at the end of the hall, and the walk seemed to last forever. The teacher saw me out in the hall, and he quickly gave the class an assignment to keep them busy. He came out to me and, since he knew who I was, skipped the greeting. He said, "We have to get a handle on his conduct. It is very disruptive to the other students." I was still clueless. I asked, "Exactly what is he doing?"

With a dramatic arm gesture, he said, "He stands up in his chair and waves to me." I didn't get the picture yet. He explained, "During a class discussion, if I don't call on him to respond, he will stand up in his chair and wave to me."

I asked, "You mean he stands up beside his desk and waves to get your attention better?" He answered, "No, he stands up on top of his chair. The other kids are losing their focus." I smiled. With a fatherly scowl, the teacher told

> COMPETITION BREEDS GOOD THINGS, AND THAT'S WHAT'S HAPPENED HERE.
>
> *Al Unser*

me that I needed to take this matter seriously or it could get my son expelled. Actually, I was taking it seriously. I was proud—seriously proud. I knew from watching him as a toddler that he was born to compete. Dax took this classroom exercise as outright competition. He stood up to stand out and maybe, in his mind, compensate for the shortness of his little arm. When the teacher asked, "Who can tell me what two plus two equals?" Dax saw this as a competition that had to be won. If you want to win, you have to be aggressive and work a little harder to win.

DISCIPLINE WITH A SMILE

I told the teacher that he was creating a competitive environment in Dax's mind, and all the teacher had to do was reword his inquiries or call on specific students so that Dax wouldn't feel he had to compete. He didn't agree with my assessment and told me to call Dax out in the hall and instruct him to change his behavior. I obliged and the teacher was pleased that he had the upper hand. Besides, what did I know about proper education techniques?

I talked seriously, but with a smile as Dax came into the hall. Proudly, I instructed him, "Keep it up. Try to stay down in your chair, but still try to be the best." I wanted to positively reinforce his aggressive behavior. What if Dax had hidden from attention? What if he was afraid to be around other kids? This was Dax's first real public interaction other than church, and they can't kick you out of church, where they have to practice patience. I knew that someday this competitive spirit would be so valuable. I smiled at him, and the teacher was annoyed with me. He thought I should have been much harsher, perhaps with my finger in Dax's face. No dad could have been prouder or more relieved than I was at that time.

I didn't hear from the teacher again. I think he realized that Dax's mind was not made to sit still either.

Chapter 5

ORGANIZED SPORTS

O rganized sports was the next step for Dax. I still wondered about his ability levels and how well he could perform. I was afraid, but I knew he was not. It was different from school, and I knew his mind was fine, thanks to his crash helmet, but sports were more than just using your brains—or were they? The competition in organized sports becomes more specialized each year. Parents pick a sport for their child, and they do it year round. Kids have a regular season team, a club team, and even personal instructors. How could my one-handed kid compete? Despite our fears, we signed up for all the sports his cousins, his "best buddies," were playing. He played it all and loved it all. He would even play three sports in college—soccer, football, and basketball.

Soccer was the first sport. It was a no-brainer; you don't use your hands. He liked it and quickly became his team's leading scorer, which created in him a hunger for scoring. Goals were supposed to be few and far between, but he liked to get two or three a game. He looked forward to the scoring celebrations more than anything.

Baseball was tougher. Dax would catch the ball, toss it up, pull off his glove, catch the ball again, and then throw it. It was a seamless process. Today, he still cannot believe people can catch the ball with their non-dominant hand and throw with the other. He was good, and we both thought he could play professionally. He watched Jim Abbott play and collected his baseball cards, but that was also the problem with baseball. It had been done before.

Football came later, and Dax excelled there too, especially in the hitting. After all, he had a lot of practice running his head into things. But football was not his favorite sport.

Dax fell in love with basketball. I wouldn't say I encouraged it, but I sure didn't discourage it. To satisfy my boys, I poured a concrete basketball slab in the backyard, and it was a regular gathering spot. With a basketball hoop on each end, the big kids would play full court games. The younger Dax liked to watch Baric, Justin, and Vanessa play basketball, but he found it hard to stand apart and not participate, so he often just toddled out and stood in the middle of the court. Many times he'd get knocked down while his brothers shouted, "Move!" Ultimately they had to pick him up and carry him off. And Dax just found his way back into the middle of traffic. To him, it was another fun part of the game.

> THE DIFFICULTIES IN LIFE ARE SUPPOSED TO MAKE US BETTER, NOT BITTER.
>
> *Author Unknown*

Dax carefully watched his siblings' moves. If the ball ever came to him, he quickly grabbed it and heaved it as hard as he could to hit some iron. Often the only thing he succeeded in doing was making the ball sail out into the pasture, forcing the older boys to chase it down. But every now and then, a shot would fall through the net.

Backyard basketball continued until nightfall.

Frustrated with the dark, the big boys decided to hoist their little brother into the tree to tie up a flood light. After it was attached, the games continued on well into the night. Every time, Dax was out in the middle of it.

Chapter 6

ADVERSITY AND DECISIONS

Dax was a good athlete by age eleven. He thrived emotionally, gained confidence, and built self-esteem as he performed well in physical activities. That year I sent him to a large university summer basketball camp, which opened on Monday and ended on Saturday. Each boy was assigned a coach for the week. When I left Dax, he seemed to be in good spirits, so I didn't make a big deal about being on his own for a whole week.

Dax called home a couple of times and let us know how he was doing. He sounded happy and positive. When I returned, I walked into the gym and saw him running up and down the floor, and I knew that he was a valuable asset to his little team, but more important, he was having a positive experience. He was making good passes and dribbling well. I asked him how many points he scored, and he quickly spouted, "Six!" His team needed him, and the coach accepted him. When the tournament was over, Dax received an all-star award for his hustle. We rode home together, Dax eyeing his trophy the whole way, and after many swings and misses with the hammer, he proudly hung it on his wall.

The following year Dax said he wanted to go back to the same camp. It was such a positive experience that we decided to send him again. Everything was the same as the year before, and we left him in good hands in the dorm room. He was a good twelve-year-old boy, and I didn't have to worry. The week passed just as it had the year before. I drove six hours from northern New Mexico to pick him up, eager to

SWEET ARE THE USES OF ADVERSITY.

Shakespeare

see the tournament. But I was late and missed everything except the last game. I walked into the gym during a

time-out and saw Dax standing alone outside of the team huddle. By the way he was standing, I knew something was wrong. When the buzzer sounded, he went to the bench and sat down. Only a few minutes were left in the game, and afterwards, they gave out the awards again. Instead of participating, Dax sat and watched this time.

CHOOSE FREEDOM, NOT ANGER

When the ceremony was over, I walked out with Dax, who was silent, to the parking lot and asked, "What's wrong?" He hung his head and explained what he had overheard that week. "Coach said that one-handed boys don't play basketball." I couldn't believe my ears. This was the first real pessimist in Dax's life, and it came from someone that I had paid to teach my son. Should I go back in and let them have it with both barrels? Should I give them a real piece of my mind? Should I wait and see how Dax would really take this?

Dax explained how the coach didn't let him participate in games and how he was instructed to "watch the other kids do it." Dax recalled what happened when the coach finally did put him into scrimmage. Dax performed a simple shot fake and went around his defender to score only to have the coach blow the whistle. The coach ran in front of the hoop to stop Dax and said patronizingly, "You're doing so great." Dax didn't understand why the coach didn't let him finish the basket. It was the first time a person stood in his way.

I decided not to go back in and argue or get a well-deserved refund because from what I had seen in my life, one-handed boys really don't play basketball. In fact, I didn't know any other one-handed people, and I felt that it was a bad example to complain or play the victim card.

We got in the car in silence. It was the loneliest ride we have ever spent. Hardly anything was said for the first five hours of the ride—five hours of pain as I watched his anger turn to hurt, disbelief, and then back to anger as he replayed the week's events in his mind.

When we reached Cortez, Colorado, we had one hour left on our ride. Dax turned to me and said, "What would happen if I got so good the coach had to play me?" I was shocked by the change of attitude. Dax had finally let it all out and had freed himself. I knew that what he meant was, "I will become the best basketball player. They can't take me out if I don't miss shots. They will see that one-handed boys can play just as good as two-handed boys."

That night Dax set a goal. "I want to play D-I basketball." I thought he didn't know what "D-I" meant. Why didn't he say professional basketball or that he wanted to be NBA MVP? It was still lofty, but I couldn't help but feel that if any boy could do it, it was my boy. The next hour was a father's dream—it was all about basketball. We talked about and planned how to make Dax's dream come true.

Chapter 7

PREPARE MENTALLY

D r. Joyce Brothers said, "It is no exaggeration to say that a strong positive self-image is the best possible preparation for success in life."[1] As his parents, we were concerned about how Dax perceived himself. We encouraged him to develop the highest self-image and prepare for the future. He seemed to naturally sense what Victor Hugo observed, "A small man is made up of small thoughts."[2] Dax did not want others to see him as a small-minded person.

With this determination to succeed, Dax decided to prepare his mind better than before. He wanted to know what great people thought when they were young, so he collected quotations from the lives of great people. He told me that he was going to copy them and put them on his bedroom wall to be reminded every day about how to improve.

Dax made several good decisions from this episode in his life. First, he chose not to make a scene when the coach didn't play him. Second, he chose not to whine or say ugly things to others because he wasn't getting what he wanted. Third, he decided to change himself instead of expecting others to change their ways or behavior. Fourth, after his emotional cleansing, he left the hurt behind. He decided to set goals for his own improvement. These decisions would help him later

> ## SUCCESS IS WHERE PREPA-RATION AND OPPORTUNITY MEET.
>
> *Bobby Unser*

when real adversity knocked on the door.

Shakespeare wrote, "Sweet are the uses of adversity."[3] These "sweet" moments occur in each of our lives, and they allow us the opportunity to define or refine our character. What kind of person will I become? Will I let others tell me who I am or what I will be? Will I allow them to influence my life and, if so, how much? Will I choose friends who will support my goals or hang out with those who will pull me down? Will I accept defeat or will I use the adversity to make myself great?

THE POWER OF WORDS

I memorized a poem by Edgar Guest and have often repeated it to my children. It was one of the first quotes to go up on Dax's wall, where he posted it next to his all-star award. This poem has power to move us and assists in character building. According to it, we don't have to play the blame game that our society plays. We can step away from the victim culture.

YOU
Edgar Guest

You are the fellow that has to decide
Whether you'll do it or toss it aside.
You are the fellow who makes up your mind
Whether you'll lead or will linger behind
Whether you'll try for the goal that's afar
Or just be contented to stay where you are.

Take it or leave it. Here's something to do!
Just think it over—It's all up to you!
What do you wish? To be known as a shirk,
Known as a good man who's willing to work,
Scorned for a loafer or praised by your chief,
Rich man or poor man or beggar or thief?
Eager or earnest or dull through the day,
Honest or crooked? It's you who must say!
You must decide in the face of the test
Whether you'll shirk it or give it your best.[4]

Dax memorized this one quickly because he had heard it so much by the time he was twelve. It had already started to sink in long before he reached his Cortez, Colorado, catharsis. Emotionally, he still struggled when someone called him handicapped because "handicapped" meant he could not do it. It equaled poor mental fitness. He knew he was different, but now he was determined to show people, especially coaches, that they needed to stop seeing him only as handicapped.

The first time I spouted, "You are the fellow that has to decide," I expected it to roll off Dax's back, but he understood and wanted more. I don't know if it was the rhythm of the poetry, the prestige of the person saying the words, or the feelings the words provoked, but he knew what I wanted him to learn. After I quoted an author, he would quickly respond with questions: "Who said that? Who was he? What happened to him? Why did he say that?" Dax wanted some comfort, some immediate experience, to carry with him. He wanted to remember that great things were always possible.

DISCIPLINE
When Dax reached the sixth grade, he had grown slightly taller than most of the boys in his class. One day, I received

a call from the school principal at Kirtland Middle School because a teacher had complained that Dax had tripped another boy in the hallway and hurt him. Dax was a boy full of uncommon energy. He might have appeared to be handicapped, but he knew how to handle himself and in many ways, he was a typical boy.

However, the little thumb on his right arm is not a normal thumb.

> I THINK OF DISCIPLINE AS THE CONTINUAL EVERYDAY PROCESS OF HELPING A CHILD LEARN SELF-DISCIPLINE.
>
> *Fred Rogers*

He had already broken it once by that time, and the calcification process brought new bone to the area, allowing it to grow thicker and stronger. Under an X-ray his little thumb appears to be a wedge with a very sharp tip. It can be used to get somebody's attention quickly. He has poked me with it a few times, and I can tell you it really does hurt. Opposing players would eventually coin the phrase when one of them was struck by this thumb as "getting Daxed."

Dax learned how to get attention by using what God had given him, but it was too much negative attention. I could not let him develop social habits that would get him into real trouble. The teacher had complained that Dax was bullying another boy and being a "smart aleck." I knew this was a good time to intervene before anything became serious. I went to the school and signed the checkout sheet, showed the attendants in the office my identification, and asked them to call my son. I waited for a moment, and Dax finally came out. He knew he was in trouble. I asked him to explain what happened, and he told me that it wasn't as bad as the teacher had made it out to be. I told Dax that I could not allow him to become something he was not meant to be. This was the hardest thing I have ever done as a parent. Even the thought of it today brings back painful memories that I hope to never create again.

After we discussed his conduct, we both had tears in our eyes, and I said, "Well, son, it looks like you better clean out your locker because you're going to military school. So, go back in and get your stuff, and I'll check you out at the office." Dax knew I was serious. It was so painful for him that he began to sob, but I was crying more.

Right at that moment, Dax completely changed his attitude. His eyes spoke something that I had not seen before. He was begging me to relent. I was serious about taking him away rather than let him be out of control. He told me that he would start treating people with respect and that he would apologize to the boy and the teacher. I knew he was being sincere, and I believed him. From that day forward, I never received a call from the schools about Dax behaving poorly. To this day, I am tremendously relieved that I did not have to take him to a military school or anything of the sort.

The Bible contains a story about a woman named Hannah who prays with all her might for God to give her a son. She prays so hard she sways back and forth, and people think she is drunk. She promises that if she has a son, she will give the boy right back to God. Why? Out of gratitude. Her desire is fulfilled, and she has a son. She waits until the baby has grown a little and has learned correct principles.

> DO UNTO YOUR CHILDREN AS YOU WISH YOUR PARENTS HAD DONE UNTO YOU!
>
> *Louise Hart*

Then she delivers him up to Eli the prophet to be trained further. She "trained up a child in the way he should go" (Proverbs 22:6).

When Dax was a teenager, I gave him a task to move

> SELF-RESPECT LEADS TO SELF-DISCIPLINE. WHEN YOU HAVE BOTH FIRMLY UNDER YOUR BELT, THAT'S REAL POWER.
>
> *Clint Eastwood*

rocks to the back of our new house to use as fill for a new driveway. He struggled with the wheelbarrow, not just because of the poor grip due to his stub, but also because he overloaded the wheelbarrow. He wanted to quickly complete the job but kept spilling the load. Finally in frustration, he stopped taking them to the back of the house and starting throwing them discus style over the road onto Mr. Zapata's side of the road. Mr. Zapata was meticulous about keeping his roadway neat and clean. He mowed it every week with care, dedication, and precision.

When I got home Mr. Zapata came over to tell me about my fine young discus thrower. I thanked him for his diligence and his help. Dax admitted throwing the rocks over the road. I was disappointed and could only think of one thing to tell him, a line from Shakespeare: "Good name in man and woman . . . is the immediate jewel of the soul."[5] I asked him if our name was better today than it was yesterday in Mr. Zapata's mind. Dax admitted that our name was not better.

MENTAL FITNESS

Adversity, discipline, responsibility, respect, and lessons on how to treat others began to shape Dax's mental preparations. He needed to be mentally stronger than other players in order to compete at the higher levels.

For thirty-five years I have been going to work in the American job market with many great people. Often I have worked two jobs at once so that Valerie could stay at home.

However, in each place there has been at least one person who feels that the best way to "help" others is to criticize them. These critics believe that their coworkers will benefit from their so called "wisdom." I disagree. The best way to help people, especially our young, is to see the best in them. Encourage them to be better. Look for that one thing that you admire in them and let it take shape. To be better, they must see some way they can improve. Telling them how they never measure up, kills their enthusiasm for life.

Every day at a luxury car dealership I pass by Jonathan, age thirty, who has an amazing ability to disassemble an automobile and put it back together even better. These cars have numerous bells, alarms, and gadgets. Last week, I stopped to look at his organized "mess" on the floor and, as I shook my head back and forth, he asked, "What?"

I questioned, "Jonathan, do you play chess?"

He answered, "No, Why?"

I replied, "You would be a great chess player. You have an amazing memory. You could anticipate several moves ahead, and that's what good chess players do."

He smiled and said that he had never thought about his job that way. I complimented Jonathan's mental fitness and ability. I see him smiling more often now.

Assembling a luxury car, producing a winning chess strategy, or devising ways to win basketball games with one hand requires mental fitness. Dax's excellent mental fitness had to precede hours of physically demanding practice. His positive self-image was taking great shape, and he would need it because we had a long journey ahead of us.

Chapter 8

THE JOURNEY BEGINS

Our first priority was finding a good place to practice indoors. We already had the huge concrete court in the backyard with two baskets, but the goals were not straight. The older boys had also lowered one of the baskets to eight and half feet where they could practice their "dunks," which was another serious distraction.

Fortunately, most of the churches in our area have what we call recreation or cultural halls built into the structures. The Navajo Tribe had also constructed gyms at the local tribal government chapter houses for youth to play basketball. These gyms give youth the opportunity to stay out of trouble and even to excel. They're a great asset for the community, and that is where we checked for gym access. Practicing outdoors was not a good idea because bad weather ruins consistency and form.

PRACTICE EXCELLENCE, NOT MEDIOCRITY

I have always abhorred mediocrity. Practicing at the level of mediocrity seemed equally absurd. If Dax was serious about his basketball dream, I was going to teach him the power of proper practice.

So much of basketball is repetition, and excellence is

> ADVERSITY HAS EVER BEEN
> CONSIDERED THE STATE IN
> WHICH A MAN MOST EASILY
> BECOMES ACQUAINTED WITH
> HIMSELF.
>
> *Samuel Johnson*

directly correlated to it. I focused on doing things the correct way, and Dax repeated it over and over. Repetition perfects two things: your muscles and your mind. Your muscles remember the correct shooting form, the timing, the speed, and the distance to make the shot. Your mind is a muscle too. Practicing gives your mind confidence to do it correctly. Many young basketball players go into a practice session perfecting their game-winning half-court shots. They then end the practice session doing the same thing. Why practice a shot that maybe comes around once in a season? Dax began to acquire my disdain for mediocrity. This was his first lesson—get real, stay real, and get good.

I was not a basketball coach and didn't have the keys to the high school gym. Our local high school had three gymnasiums, but all were locked in the evenings except when a local man was bent on obtaining state championship banners for the girl's program. If he was in the gym with the girls, Dax and I could usually find a way in and use a corner of a gym without the alarms going off. I begged several teachers and coaches for a key, but I was not "certified."

PRAISE AND GRATITUDE

Our most consistent venue at this time became the churches. We begged janitors at the churches for time to practice during the winter. Often, they would oblige. Some of the "gyms" had carpet on the floors, but it was better than concrete or snow. The custodians sometimes got irritated, but we tried to leave the place clean and ready for the next "beggars." As we left the building, we would effusively thank the custodians for their patience and hard work. Before we left I made it my goal to make them smile. (One time, Dax even sat down and had lunch with one of the custodians.) I would compliment them on how nice and clean the church was. It was much better to leave the place with them happy than wondering if that would be our last invitation.

Dax needed to dribble on the basketball court under any circumstance. I knew from my own experience that a high school coach would not put him on the floor if he could not dribble well at all times. Shooting would come later. Dunking was not even on the radar screen. I had Dax dribble the length of the floor with his stub. This gave him amazing confidence. Dax next dribbled the ball going back and forth from hand to stub. Then he practiced turning around without losing any momentum or the ball.

The ultimate test came when I asked Dax to dribble between his legs. He easily lost the ball between his legs, coming back from stub to hand. Dax's older sister, Vanessa, was a part of the girl's varsity program, so I had her demonstrate how to dribble the length of the floor between her legs. Vanessa was very good, and Dax had to practice quite a while before he mastered that skill. The greatest challenge came when Vanessa dribbled all around the gym between her legs without stopping. She made every 90-degree turn without muffing the dribble. Dax struggled mightily. He would lose the ball after four or five passes between his legs. He was so angry with himself at times that he often wanted to kick the ball and send it flying. Several times he did let it sail across the gym. This was probably why his

> PRACTICE—VICTORIOUS WARRIORS WIN FIRST AND THEN GO TO WAR.
>
> *Sun Tzu*

soccer foot became so lethal during his high school years, but I knew that his anger was not really directed at the ball. In reality, his anger was directed at anybody who said, "One-handed boys don't play basketball."

Disappointment during hard practices led to introspection: "Can I really do this? Do I really want to put in that much time at this?" His anger was understandable, but it needed to be conditioned and pointed in the right direction. He had to express those powerful emotions without being destructive.

> SUCCESS CONSISTS OF GOING FROM FAILURE TO FAILURE WITHOUT LOSS OF ENTHUSIASM.
>
> *Winston Churchill*

A healthy, out loud conversation cleaned up his emotions whether the conversation was with me or himself. The introspection, sweat, and hard practice led to epiphany after epiphany. This was where he could not lie to himself. This was when he had to say to himself, "I can do this, but I will need to practice harder. I will have to bear being shown up by my older sister, and I will have to tolerate Dad watching me with a hawk eye every time I fail."

Sometimes I thought we would be kicked out of the churches because of the noise the ball made when it hit the walls. (In fact, several times we were asked to leave the building when a meeting, baptism, or party was set to happen.) Frustration and disappointment were necessary or Dax would fail. I felt it was good for him to vent after each failure, but with each try, his skills gradually improved. Often, he would stop to examine the "baby fingers" on his stub and wipe the blood off on his trunks or sweats. He abhorred tape or band aids on his stub because it reduced his already limited sense of touch. I often wondered if he would simply "throw in the towel," but it never happened. Determination and dedication mixed with a good measure of healthy anger and a love for the game became his drive for success.

Dax watched every available basketball movie from "The Movie Barn," a big red barn packed to the brim with VHS movies. He watched any and all things basketball; then, he ran outside to practice the moves of Pistol Pete, Michael Jordan, John Stockton, or any of the Spectacular Guards of the NBA. He loved the magic of ball handling.

Eventually, Vanessa showed how to do the stationary switch legs dribble. While standing in the same spot and putting a foot forward with each dribble, she passed the ball between her legs to the other hand. She did it twenty plus times before she stopped. Dax was unable to master the delicacy and smoothness that this skill required and that a girl naturally displays. It was another challenge he had to secretly be irritated by for the next few years, but eventually he reached her skill level.

On one occasion, I overheard one of the custodians say, "Can you believe what he is making that poor boy go through?" Actually it was the other way around. Dax was putting me through the workout. I tried to keep up with him, but I understood what it must have looked like to them, especially if they looked at Dax's bleeding stub. He practiced dancing with the ball. Multiple spin moves, behind the back dribbles, between the leg passes—anything to make himself unstoppable.

Basketball is a game of finesse. Not only did Dax learn to handle the ball, he developed a polished touch, even though his sense of touch was limited. It took him longer to learn, with more repetitions, but it came. I knew that dribbling could be his Achilles heel to an unforgiving high school coach, so we practiced this skill almost to perfection.

SCORING

Most boys dream of being the scorer—the finisher—and Dax was no different. He quickly learned that the headline in the local paper would never read, "Crum Scores None in Win." He wanted to score. All the dribbling practice helped him to get the basket and finish. He was good at attacking from anywhere. Right side, left side, down the middle—he had moves from everywhere. He often stood on the three point line, took one dribble, and finished on the other side of the hoop. His left hand was big, and he used it to spin the ball off the backboard on either side to make shots.

Shooting was his favorite. Short distances were easy, but how do one-handed players become good at the "magical" three-pointer? The answer—he would shoot them all day. The three-pointer is a game winner and game loser. (I wish it had been implemented in 1972 when I played against Reserve.) The three-pointer is useful drama. It can sway the momentum toward the small player. You can impressively dunk for two points, but I can win with my smooth snap of the wrist and follow-through for three points. Each of these skills made Dax more complete and more dynamic. One hand or two, he was a formidable opponent for any other kid in the state.

But there was something much more important—free throws. Players who shoot free throws well are finishers, and coaches want them on the floor at the end of the game. A good ball player receives enough fouls at first to stop him and then eventually harder fouls to keep him from getting up. Dax would finish his last collegiate season at SUU with a 94.7 free throw percentage, beating the current NCAA basketball record of 94.57 percent. This season record did not stand because he had too few attempts.

I would stand under the basket and pop the ball back to Dax every day, and I mean *every day*. Free throws were first priority on shooting. He didn't let up until he made ninety-two

in a row one day.
His left arm built
great shooting
strength. Then
we went for nine-
teen-footers. I
had him do just as

> I'VE FAILED OVER AND OVER
> AND OVER AGAIN IN MY LIFE
> AND THAT IS WHY I SUCCEED.
>
> *Michael Jordan*

his sister did. We established seven different stations around the arc, where he had to make a basket before he could go to the next. As soon as he could make one from each place around the arch, we went up to two at each station. If he couldn't make them in a row, he couldn't go to the next spot. Before he stopped practicing at the high school level, he was making five in a row from each spot. Once, during his senior year in high school, Dax stopped at his favorite spot and made twenty in a row, a skill he carried into college.

We finished each practice with some kind of resistance or aerobic workout. We couldn't afford weights, expensive club memberships, or home exercise equipment. When Dax's older brothers were involved in sports, we bought some bungee cords and made pulling devices and lifting tools so they could begin resistance training. Combined with home exercises, Dax's jumping ability dramatically increased.

As Dax and I recall our journey, one thing he hopes for all kids—and not just those who are born different—to know is that success is never immediate and never defined by one moment in your life. Success is in the journey. When you stop moving forward, your success stops too. Delayed gratification is a dying philosophy. If kids don't see success immediately, they revert to their mediocre ways—give up. They never see real success, which is seeing what hard work can accomplish, what hard work can overcome over time. Dax's skills were not accomplished overnight. He was born without a hand and without skills, but neither could stop him from becoming great.

Chapter 9

FRESHMAN BASKETBALL

Dax was growing up. He'd already had many "grown-up" experiences, which he'd handled very maturely, but now he was moving into high school. I decided to retire from working at the power plant and became the junior varsity basketball coach of Kirtland Central High School. As a freshman, Dax played on my high school junior varsity team and became a legitimate starter for the team. Three high school juniors were on the team and several sophomores played alongside him. Our team was successful and well disciplined, with a winning record going into the Christmas break. A tournament was scheduled in Pagosa Springs, Colorado, with three other JV teams, and we knew we had a good chance of winning.

The first game was against a southern Colorado team, Montezuma Cortez High School. Yeah, that's right. Cortez—where Dax became Dax. Cortez was bigger than us, but I knew we had boys that could bring home the tournament trophy. We played well in the first half, and the other team was frustrated with their inability to stay with our full court fast break. At half time, we were up twenty points. The second half started out physically with some pushing and jostling. I was begging the referees to watch the game

> GREAT ACHIEVEMENT IS USUALLY BORN OF GREAT SACRIFICE.
>
> *Napoleon Hill*

closer and call more fouls. Players that opposed Dax often took offense to the fact that a one-handed player was beating them. My pleas to the refs did little good. The big boys in the other jerseys were easily pushing us around, but we were beating them even more on the scoreboard, which made them even more frustrated.

Hard foul followed hard foul. On one drive down the floor, Dax went in for a layup, and the biggest boy on the other team caught Dax around the neck and laid him out. You could hear his elbows and face hit the hardwood floor. Dax rose from the floor grabbing his mouth. His two front teeth were bloody and were pointing straight backwards. He reached in and pulled his front teeth back down, oblivious to what was going on behind him.

CLIFTON'S HONOR

Clifton Yazzie, a stout Navajo boy and our center, had had enough of the Cortez center, who obviously needed a lesson in manners. Clifton shoved the opposing player away from Dax. The benches cleared as several players from both teams gathered around and restrained them. Clifton was ready to sacrifice his playing time for Dax's honor. None of my boys were fighters, but Clifton knew there was a point to where patience should give way to respect. Dax learned that year that he could count on Clifton to come to his aid and honor. Clifton and Dax admired each other's spirit and drive to succeed. The referees dismissed Clinton and the Cortez center from the game, and Dax continued playing. Clifton came and sat down by me and continued to encourage our team. He didn't apologize for his actions, but I never expected him to because to me his actions were full of selflessness and had a good measure of nobility.

SELFLESS SACRIFICE

Clifton and Dax both made the varsity team the next year. Clifton was a senior, and he wanted to make it his best. Throughout the entire year, Clifton was a substitute and played with the permanent defense, so the starters could have something to work against. Meanwhile, my junior varsity team was just too small and slow. Dax made the starting five and went up against larger and stronger players every game. Clifton continued to sacrifice his desire to play while the starters were interviewed by the media.

Kirtland Central High School hadn't won a state championship in boy's basketball since 1978. It was 2001, and it had been a twenty-three year drought for blue trophies. In the first round of the playoffs, our starters played miserably and fouled out. We were losing to Artesia, New Mexico, the way many teams had lost for years. The game was winding down, and it wasn't looking good. Dax fouled out, and Coach Scott sent Clifton into the game. An Artesia player came in for a layup. Clifton stood still and let the opponent completely run over him. This is very unique in basketball. In football, hockey, and baseball, it is legal to run over an opponent in many situations. In basketball, it's called taking a charge. In life, it's called selfless sacrifice. His willingness to sacrifice gave new life to our team, and his enthusiasm spread to all our players. The comeback was underway, and Pat Crawford's

> YOU WERE BORN TO WIN, BUT TO BE A WINNER, YOU MUST PLAN TO WIN, PREPARE TO WIN, AND EXPECT TO WIN.
>
> *Zig Ziglar*

45-foot half court shot sent the game into overtime so that we could win. The ten-hour bus ride home didn't feel that long because the team had learned how to come back when defeat was so close. We had renewed hopes of winning in Albuquerque.

Dax learned from that game another skill that would later help him to excel: the Clifton Concept—sacrifice comfort and put your desires second so together everyone can win. This came in handy when he got to college. Clifton showed how to not be a team cancer, someone who is a discourager—a teammate who bad-mouths the coach, the program, the other teammates—until the whole program dies from the inside out.

WHAT IS A WINNER?

Clifton graduated with the other seniors, spent some time at home, and then enlisted in the army and was deployed to Iraq. He sent home pictures of himself and his team on patrol in a Hummer. He called me twice on a special military phone that they could only use at certain times.

The first time he called, I asked if he had called his mother. He said that he was going to call her right after he talked to me. I asked why he called me first and why he didn't show more respect to his mother. He said, "Coach, I want to thank you for all the time you gave me and how you made me believe in myself. I will never forget playing on your team. We had more fun that year than I'd ever had." I thanked Clifton for his example to the rest of the team and to me. He then said, "Coach, did you say that I was an example to you?" I replied, "Yes, Clifton. Your example is what winners are made of. Without players like you, championship caliber teams never reach their potential. Somebody had to give up his comfort and time. Some players have to hurry while they wait. Some have to hustle while they wait.

Everybody wants to be a starter, and nobody wants to be a supporter or substitute. What coaches need are finishers, not starters."

Clifton came home from Iraq to visit several teammates, and we took pictures. I asked him what he was going to do with the rest of his life. With a firm, serious, and most determined reply, Clifton looked at me and said, "Coach, this is my life. I'm going back to Iraq."

"Cliff, do you know the risk?"

"Yes, Coach, I know all the risks. This is my life."

Two months later, I received a phone call from a woman who could barely speak. At first, I could not understand who was on the line, but I knew somebody was there. In a broken, small voice that came from a sweet Navajo lady, she said, "Coach . . . Clifton . . . was killed in Iraq." She asked me to speak at a memorial service at the Farmington, New Mexico, civic center. At the memorial I spoke of the traits of a true champion. I told the crowd of several thousand why Clifton was a champion—his selfless example and his willingness to continue to sacrifice. Beforehand, the crowd knew very little of how Clifton had sacrificed on the junior varsity and varsity basketball teams, but when they realized that in the army Clifton was simply continuing to give up his comfort for others, his life made sense. He didn't have to take a charge in basketball or charge into Iraq, but Clifton's noble actions are not so senseless now.

MASTERING THE CLIFTON CONCEPT

In Dax's final year playing for Southern Utah University, he was finally elevated to the level of starter for the team, and they started to win. To many people, it didn't make sense. How could the addition of a one-handed basketball player initiate more wins? What is it that makes the difference?

I once drove eight hours from Mesa, Arizona, to watch

Dax play. His wife, Ashley, told me how frustrating it was to know that if the coaches would just put Dax in the game, the team would win. Before Dax became a starter for that team, they had won less than one-fourth of their games. When Dax became a starter, the team won eight out of ten games. During the game, I noticed Dax was one of the two smallest players on the floor. Often, it was Dax's role to set a screen on one of the bigger players so that his teammate could get open for a shot or pass. Several times Dax was simply run over, and he had to pull himself out from underneath a pile of tall bodies. Each time he quickly got back into the action and was ready to go again.

Seeing his sacrifice and determination to succeed gave me enthusiasm to cheer even harder, and his teammates caught fire with him. Players on both teams often sacrificed their comfort on offense, especially when they had the ball in their hands, but when the ball went to the other team their intensity fell dramatically. Many looked like they were taking a break and even relaxing. When I looked at Dax, I noticed that his intensity never left. As Fox Sports said, "He was an absolute hound on defense." He had mastered the Clifton Concept and improved it.

Chapter 10

DAVID AND GOLIATH

In 2001, during Dax's sophomore year in high school, our basketball team made it to the state playoffs. We had a better chance than the year before when we had lost to Los Alamos, New Mexico. Los Alamos had a player whose size intimidated us the year before. At seven feet tall, he could dunk the ball standing flat-footed. They also had the biggest high school team I have ever seen in New Mexico.

During regular varsity games I became an assistant varsity coach beside Coach Scott. However, during tournament play I became our team scout and I was sent to Espanola to scout Los Alamos. The more my scouting pen wrote, the more I knew that we could beat them. We needed to keep ourselves in the game, stay out of foul trouble, and remain close until the end. Kenny, our six-foot-two middle linebacker, had to guard their seven-footer. He needed to meet him at the top of the key and keep him out of the paint. Zach, our six-foot-four center, could guard their power forward, who was at six foot six. They had a starting point guard who was six foot four while our starting point guard, Pat, was five foot eight. Dax, six foot two, had to guard their six-foot-five shooting guard. When we measured up, their height advantage would be a combined twenty-seven inches—over two feet. Terron, six foot, and Devon, six foot three, would guard six-foot-six players also. Devon was only a freshman.

We exited the Pit dressing room next to where the University of New Mexico Lobos and now the Los Alamos Hilltoppers had dressed. We felt the anxiety of the long walk down the ramp leading to the floor, where amazingly Jim Valvano's North Carolina State team beat Houston. Michael Jordan once said that he hated half time at the Pit because he hated to walk back up that ramp. A trash can placed just where the concrete begins its descent is used not so much for trash as it is for nervous athletes to empty their stomach contents. A packed house would often produce so much noise that car alarms in the parking lot would be set off and fans' eardrums would rupture, sending blood down the sides of their faces. It was indeed an intimidating place.

Our boys stopped to huddle and have their usual group shout and to retie their shoes, if needed. Dax stooped down to tie his shoes better and untied one shoe. Kenny saw Dax tie his shoe, but Dax did it so quickly that Kenny couldn't believe what he had seen. He told the team to stop. He bent down and untied Dax's shoe and said, "Hey, do that again. I've never seen that before." Dax was an underclassman and had to do what the big boys told him, so he obediently tied his shoe again. Kenny still couldn't believe that a one-handed boy tied his shoe so quickly. Kenny then said, "How did I miss that all this year? It's amazing." It was such a positive moment to take their minds off what awaited them on the floor. All the Davids paused for a moment before meeting the Goliaths, and the diversion kept the boys from throwing up in the trash can that year.

CAN-DO ATTITUDE
The shoe-tying minute was a gratitude and a can-do attitude moment. It had the same effect on my English classes

when I invited Dax to show the students how a one-handed boy ties his shoes. Many students just stared and were afraid to speak. The bold always asked for another showing. The students never came forward to challenge him to a shoe-tying contest for speed. Why were they so amazed to watch a one-handed boy tie his shoes? First, we want to believe that our way is the right way, and here is someone who is challenging how we think. Second, our minds resist change.

> CHOOSE WELL; YOUR CHOICE IS BRIEF, AND YET ENDLESS.
>
> *Johann Wolfgang von Goethe*

Change is uncomfortable because it makes us adjust, stretch, and even ache. When Dax ties his shoes, it is like a magician performing an act, but it is real and nothing is faked. The students asked to see it three, four, and five times. Once wasn't good enough—just like Kenny untying Dax's shoe and saying, "Tie that again." It was a positive replay.

Positive quotes strengthen minds and build resolve. Affirmative messages provide a solid foundation from which to build a strong character. Eleanor Roosevelt spoke to Dax every night, "Nobody can make you feel inferior without your consent."[1] Dr. Martin Luther King's voice in "I have a dream"[2] was stronger than the distractions; those words told Dax to never let go of his dream. Winston Churchill's admonition to "Never give in, never give in"[3] was so powerful that the other voices could not be heard. He had never heard nor seen Eleanor, Martin, or Winston, but he felt he knew what special people they must have been—people who experienced hard times.

"I WILL GO"

In the Old Testament, David approaches Saul and says, "Let no man's heart fail because of him, I will go" (see 1 Samuel 17:32). David agreed to fight the nine-foot-tall

Gath giant, Goliath. John Wayne said it best though—
"Courage is being scared to death, but saddling up anyway."[4]
Our small team walked down the ramp to play some very
large young men.

Somehow we went into overtime and got their big man
fouled out of the game. With six seconds left, Dax guarded
their leading scorer in the backcourt. A quick jab left Dax
in the dust. He turned and raced back in front to contest
the game winning shot. Los Alamos missed. Kirtland High
School finally won.

How do you stop a seven-foot, 250-pound future division one basketball player headed for the Mountain West
Conference? With a six-foot-two, 230-pound future Division
I linebacker also headed for the Mountain West Conference.
Kenny ended the game with fifteen points, twelve rebounds,
and four blocked shots. Kenny is not a small person, but
often during the game it was hard to see him. You could
see a big Los Alamos player being scooted out of the paint,
but we would not have won that game without Dax and
Devon, a sophomore and a freshman. We rotated them into
the game to help double-team the seven-footer.

ENCOURAGEMENT COUNTS
After the tournament, I watched the videotapes of the
tournament games and was amazed at how many times
Kenny offered words of encouragement to Dax and Devon.
He even put his arm around them a couple of times to reas-
sure them that they were valued and needed. His reassur-
ances were a powerful voice to the two young players, who
were playing in the Pit for the first time. His actions gave
both of them permission to play with their best and to excel.

Chapter 11

NO DOUBT ABOUT IT!

S hakespeare wrote, "Our doubts are traitors and make us lose the good we oft' might win by fearing to attempt."[1] Can doubts and fear make us lose? Yes. Doubts are in great supply today. We doubt a marriage will succeed. We doubt our national economy can recover. We doubt politicians can be honest. It was no different when we got to this championship game. No one believed the small town boys could beat the perennial champions.

Los Alamos was the biggest, and we beat them by getting physical and getting them in foul trouble. Academy was the most skilled team, and we were going to be tested by their offensive skills and defensive tenacity. Newspapers all over the state ran articles advising us that we were going up against the best program in the state of New Mexico. During the 1990s Mike Brown of Albuquerque Academy had engineered a string of six 4A state championships. He always had his boys in top condition, well muscled, and superbly disciplined in order to carry out his unique, winning program. His tenacious defenses caused other teams to give up quickly. The newspapers said we were "lucky" to have slipped past the Los Alamos giants, and now we would experience the humility that comes from taking on the tenacity and strength of a top-notch opponent that regularly sends players to the college ranks.

Never "Fear to Attempt"

What the media never knew was how the last two wins had transformed our players' attitudes. When Kenny constantly reinforced Dax's and Devon's efforts during the Los Alamos game, it gave our "puppies" unbelievable confidence. To a freshman and sophomore, a senior's green light means even more than the coach's approval. A coach can sit you down to discipline you or correct your efforts, but a solid senior's smile and pat on the back takes away all doubts. Four seniors approving a sophomore's efforts meant we were indeed a team.

Respect Your Opponents

We had tremendous respect for Mike Brown's Chargers, but we never feared them. People didn't expect us to even stay up with his perennial powerhouse charges. We were supposed to bow out early because of our seventh place ranking. But we had already experienced walking down the ramp to about seven thousand fans that hovered over us. Three thousand more did not seem that frightening, and many would be from Kirtland. Our game plan was to, without fail, know where their top shooter and Division I–bound shooting guard was at all times. His three-pointers could easily take us out of the game, and then we would be chasing Chargers around the floor in a stall game. If we could keep their shooter distracted and win the fight under the backboards, we could win.

Academy had shut down our district rival Farmington with a great defense in the semifinals, and now we were facing it. Coach Scott implemented a slide zone defense, and it caused Academy some trouble, but their good shooting overcame our hustle. We started slow and were behind 14–6. After the first quarter, we changed to a "box and one" defense to keep track of their great shooter. Four guys protect the basket while one player chases the shooter. The media people behind us called it a "gimmick" defense, but it worked better and better with each possession. Terron was assigned to stay on their shooter, and their shots began to miss. Pat and Dax concentrated on offense and the defensive perimeter.

With 5:23 remaining in the fourth quarter, Academy's starting guard hit two foul shots. Academy led 43–40 and had great momentum. Although their next possessions were scoreless, we still had to catch up when we got the ball back. We worked the ball around, when suddenly Dax stood all alone on the three-point line above the key. It was as if the entire Academy team had forgotten about him. Did they not respect his ability to shoot threes? He caught a pass from the other side of the floor and shot a clean three-pointer. A Charger flew to block Dax's shot and knocked Dax to the floor just as the ball went through the hoop. The game was tied. Two of our seniors ran to the arc, picked Dax up, and practically carried him to the free throw line where the other two seniors met him. They all had smiles of confidence in a team huddle, but Dax missed the free throw, so we were still tied. I flashed back to my missed layup thirty years ago against Reserve. But there was still time enough for the team to win.

Academy had two more possessions and missed both attempts. Dax was fouled again, and we were in the bonus. He made his next four free throws. Dax had done it. My doubts quickly vanished. We took the lead for good with 1:39 to play. Academy cut the lead to 45–44 in a free throw shooting contest. After that we scored eight more unanswered free throws to win the game 53–44. Dax finished the game with fourteen points, leading the team.

When the game was winding down and Dax was shooting foul shots, one of the announcers behind me said, "Wow, no doubt about it, this boy is a legitimate player. He can really play."

LOSE WITH DIGNITY, WIN WITH CLASS

Legendary baseball manager Casey Stengel remarked, "You gotta lose 'em some of the time. When you do, lose 'em right."[2] We all experience loss, but how we lose often defines who we are much more than winning. We don't have to train to lose, but we can train ourselves to lose properly.

Albuquerque Academy taught us how a quality program can lose with decency and dignity. There were no hard feelings or words. In fact, the following year when we made it to the playoffs again, Coach Brown invited us to their campus to use their facilities to prepare for the tournament. In one of those sessions, Coach Brown paid me a great compliment. When I walked into their gym, he came toward me and asked, "Is Dax your son?"

"Yes, sir."

"Why didn't you tell me? He absolutely tore us up last year."

There was only respect for each other's teams. His voice and actions showed respect and dignity. To this day, I continue to have great respect for his coaching ability and the example he is to all of New Mexico. Opponents do not have to be enemies. Respect and dignity do not have to be left out of sports.

Dax strives to never let doubts or fears control his emotions. I have never seen a player that has been able to put fear into him. Fear allows other players to manipulate you. Respect and decency are emotional armor, and he needed to be hard-shelled to beat the crowds, media, and opponents in life's contests.

Dax taught me that winning is not a matter of how big I am physically or how many times I have won in the past. Victor Hugo said, "People don't lack strength, they lack will."[3] Winning is having the will to prepare to win. Winning is accomplished before the game ever begins. It is overcoming obstacles and jumping over or knocking down another hurdle. Winning is mastering another skill when everyone says that you can't do it: "You have the wrong skin color. You are too short. You only have one hand. One-handed boys don't play baseball. One-handed boys can't catch a football." Winning is showing two-handed boys how to hit twenty three-pointers in a row. Winning is removing all doubts from your mind and your opponents' minds. Winning is holding the trophy high above your head every day, even if it is only in your heart.

To show their appreciation, the community booster club bought each of the team members state championship rings. Each team member received a ring—starters, substitutes, bench warmers, and coaches. Some of the boys who had complained about sitting on the bench now saw how their sacrifice had paid off. They were champions too. They weren't just substitute champions or benchwarmer champions. The patience they maintained was as difficult to endure as the exhaustion was for the starters.

Chapter 12

"KEEP YOUR HEAD"

fter the first state championship in 2001 and the celebration in the Pit was over, the security people quickly moved fans off the floor and ushered everyone out of that large hole in the ground. For some reason, I did not go up the ramp with the team. I turned and started walking up the steps. To reach the concourse, thirty big concrete steps have to be conquered. As I reached about the twentieth step, I noticed I had a shadow. Someone was matching me step for step and was too close for comfort. When I turned around, my junior varsity center, Derrick, was right behind me, his eyes pleading with me. I actually thought he was going to cry. I stopped, but he said nothing. I'd proceeded again when he tapped me on the shoulder.

I gave him a minute because he could hardly speak, and then he quietly whispered, "Coach, I want to be on this team next year." He didn't stop there. He then said something very important: "Coach, what do I need to do?"

That was a very important thing for him to say. Derrick got some playing time on my JV team, but he and I both knew that he was not good enough for Coach Scott to put on the floor. In fact, his skills were so poor that he even recognized how much improvement he needed. Nobody had told him, "You are hopelessly pathetic."

It's important not to lie to young people and give them false hopes. (Many of Dax's coaches felt they were doing this with him.) I did not lie to Derrick. "Derrick, right now you don't have the skills to play in the Pit. If you want to play here you'll have to dedicate your

> **WINNING TAKES TALENT; TO REPEAT TAKES CHARACTER.**
>
> *John Wooden*

energy and effort, and you'll have to sacrifice a lot of time to make it. I believe you can make it, but it will not be easy. Are you willing to do what it takes?"

Then he said something scary: "Coach, I will do anything you tell me to." He was frustrated with himself and how he had performed that past year, and I had his complete trust. I was amazed at how much he was willing to devote, but I told him we would see when the time came to practice.

Derrick did everything I told him to do. His love for the game grew every day, and that love would consume his dreams. When Dax and I sneaked away to the gym, Derrick was there and ready to go. He saw how hard Dax applied himself and matched him step for step. His work ethic was so good, he would leave the gym with his gym trunks dripping sweat. The game, practice, work, and sweat became his life. Dax and Derrick pushed each other to excel.

I gave Derrick an off-season program, and he told me he would follow it to the utmost degree. I saw him several times to check up on him. His legs became stronger and his emotional maturity grew to match. I asked him how his shot was coming, and he said that he was ready to compete. Several boys on the returning team said they had seen his workouts, and they knew he had a new love.

When the next season rolled around, Derrick was the

first on the floor and the last to leave. His intensity matched anybody on the floor. He was disgusted with himself if he missed shots. He became a team leader. His emotional game matched his new physical mastery. Coach Scott put Derrick on the floor, and he started in the position that Kenny Smith had occupied. Kenny was six foot two and 220 pounds. Derrick was only six foot and not even 180 pounds, but he was playing just like he was as big as Kenny.

LEARN FROM EXAMPLE

Derrick had improved so much that we put him in the center of the zone defense to start between Dax and Devon. One newspaper referred to Dax and Devon as the "Dynamic Duo." Every team we played was taller and more muscled than us, but our boys were tough. Derrick improved so much in his shooting that he shot 9 for 9 in a losing effort against Gallup during a tournament game where Dax and Devon struggled.

We had won a state championship, but that didn't mean much to hungry young opponents who knew that they could knock us off our throne. In the first round of the play-offs in Dax's junior year, we played a private school team in Albuquerque named St. Pius X that perennially polishes athletes to almost perfection. We had to play in their gym in front of their fans. As the boys warmed up for the game, several opposing hecklers sat behind our coaching bench so that they could tell us how bad we were going to lose and continually encouraged us to quit. With each missed shot or errant pass, these fans vehemently reminded us of our weaknesses and inabilities. In the first half of the game, we resembled the Rio Grande Zoo when the workers let all the animals loose.

St. Pius ran a great play just as the clock ticked off the last second of the first half, and a sweet little jumper gave them two points and a tremendous momentum starting the second half. Our team went to the dressing room feeling stressed. When the second half began, two of our boys could not come out because their stomachs were not cooperating. We started the half with two subs on the floor while the two starters purged.

Despite these challenges, the second half was ours. We employed a fast break scheme (commonly known as "Rez Ball" because we lived next to the large Navajo reservation), and we won the game by twenty points. The game ended, and the hecklers were gone. When did they leave? The media interviewed Devon Manning, Chase Hathaway, and Dax, the three team cousins.

WHAT'S REALLY IMPORTANT?

While Dax talked to the media, an eight-year-old boy slowly walked onto the floor, and as he stood behind Dax, I could tell that he was hiding his left hand in his pocket. He looked up at Dax and waited patiently. I slowly moved toward him, and when I got two feet from him, he looked at me.

I said to him, "Hi, I'm Dax's dad." The fear in his face told me he wanted to run away, but he was determined to stay and talk to Dax. I asked, "Can I see your hand?" The fear left his face, surprise taking its place. He slowly pulled his "hand" out of his pocket and brought a short arm that stopped at his elbow from behind his back.

I dropped to one knee and looked at his stub. It had two small fingers on it, and I asked, "How can you use these?" The expression on his face turned to relief, and he relaxed. He said, "I do a lot with it." I told him that Dax only had a small thumb on his stub, and he said, "I know. I read about him." I told him that Dax didn't walk around with his stub in his pocket, and he always tried to use it.

After the reporter finished talking to Dax, a tall, large man tapped Dax on the shoulder. After such a heated game,

IF YOU BELIEVE IN YOURSELF AND HAVE DEDICATION AND PRIDE—AND NEVER QUIT— YOU'LL BE A WINNER. THE PRICE OF VICTORY IS HIGH BUT SO ARE THE REWARDS.

Paul Bryant

Dax didn't know whether to expect a punch or a handshake. The man wanted Dax to tell his son that "he could do it." I had actually been talking to this man's son.

Dax turned around, put his stub on the boy's head, rubbed his hair, and said, "Hi." They talked for a moment, and Dax asked if there was anything that the boy couldn't do. With pride all over his face, the boy said, "If you can do it, so can I." They walked off the floor together. Waiting at the exit was a smiling, proud mother, who felt gratitude for the confidence her son had gained from watching and talking to Dax. This encounter was more important than the win or the game. A kind word at the right time can turn a life around.

We had a week off to recuperate from the game at St. Pius, and we needed it. Once more we would have to play in the Pit against the perennially powerful football town of Artesia, New Mexico. As we watched game films, I wondered if we would survive physically. We always counted on Artesia to bring big, thick, muscled bodies to the floor.

FIRST THINGS FIRST

Many teams are intimidated going from small, rural gyms to big open spaces like the Pit, and the players need as much exposure as possible if they are to "keep their heads." We had several players on the team who never got onto the floor the year before. The returning state champions are invited to sit in the Lobos locker room. Before the game, we sat on the leather couches and told the boys, "As soon as security gets off the floor, you guys get on and start shooting." Our coaching staff thought this would help them to overcome the pregame stomach butterflies and build confidence in their shots.

Because Dax consistently managed to get fouls and playing time, Artesia focused on stopping Devon during the game. Devon had the biggest build and was our leading scorer. The game was hard fought during the entire first half, and every time Devon tried to accomplish something he had a large "bulldog" in a bright orange jersey blocking his way. Artesia was formidable, and they never backed down. When the game was over, all of our players who made it onto the floor were battered and exhausted. We won the game 73–54. Dax scored twenty-two points by shooting a perfect 9 of 9 from the floor.

The championship game was against Las Cruces Onate High School, another team that was bigger and taller than us. We built up a surprising ten-point lead in the first half. The game was well played by both teams, but in the second half Onate's three-point shooter hit some critical baskets to pull the Onate Knights ahead. With seventeen points, including 10 of 13 free throws, Dax fouled out of the game, and Onate moved ahead of us. We started to see the win disappear, and Dax felt helpless on the bench.

We were down by nine points and had to fight back hard to get within one point—68–69. It would be our ball at half court. We got the ball to Devon at the top of the key, and Onate decided to double-team him at the free throw line. Devon spotted Chase, Dax's other cousin, under the hoop all alone. Chase put the ball in the basket, and we were up 70 to 69. Onate had one last chance to win with a full court pass to their big man, but the shot was off the mark. The buzzer sounded, the fans erupted, and we flew off the bench to celebrate a repeat championship. Devon scored twenty-five points, Chase scored fifteen, and Derrick Woody scored thirteen points, including the first two points of the game. Derrick was the most improved player that we had coached in our eight years at Kirtland High School boys basketball.

The boys left the Pit as champions again. Their cheering fans welcomed them with open arms, and the boys signed twice as many autographs. Don't ask me why anybody wanted these teenagers' signatures. Dax's mom was not among the screaming fans; she was too exhausted to fight the crowd to see her son, so she waited in the car.

"If you can keep your head" is a phrase from Rudyard Kipling's poem "If."[1] Many young men went off to World War I reciting those lines. It has just as much meaning for us in our day. Many people, young and old, are losing their heads in different ways—drugs, gambling, smoking, alcohol, pornography, and laziness. All these and many more are "head losing" negatives. The dark side has numerous pitfalls.

Even though Dax has an apparent disability, his overwhelming advantage has been his ability to keep his head. Dax fouled out several times in high school games, but it was because he was always giving maximum effort. In the referee's opinions he was too close, too physical, or too fast compared to the other players, and they would call fouls on him, but it never slowed him down or changed his focus.

Chapter 13

HEED THEM NOT

Dax was now a senior in high school and had been a starter on two state championship teams. Montezuma Cortez High School had been dropped from our schedule due to previous brawling encounters you could barely call basketball games (such as Dax's teeth-smashing foul). They had just won the state championship in Colorado and were on a thirty-one game winning streak. Kirtland's coaching staff spoke with their coaching staff many times about a big championship game between New Mexico and Colorado. It was risky to start the season off against a powerhouse, especially one as big and as physical as Cortez. Usually Kirtland started the season with a confidence-boosting game, but we decided it was more important to keep the level of competition high, so we agreed to play as long as the game was in our home arena.

One of Dax's distant cousins was playing for their team. He was more talented than Dax and almost as ornery. The game started as a three-point shooting contest between the two. The game was back and forth until the third quarter. Cortez went cold as we went up by about ten points. They couldn't make up the difference, and the game turned into a foul fest. The cousin outscored Dax by two points, but we won the game. We had played good team basketball.

Going into this season, we knew that a repeat state championship is more than most coaches and teams can ever dream of. At Kirtland Central High School, banner after banner of state championships are hung

> **KEEP YOUR HEAD WHEN OTHERS ARE LOSING THEIRS.**
>
> *Rudyard Kipling*

around the gym, but most of them are for girls basketball. My 1972 white runner-up banner starts off the display way over in the corner. In 1978 the boys won the championship, but it often got lost among fourteen other girls' state championships and several runner-up banners. But this time, the boys had mustered a repeat banner. How should this be celebrated? What to do with another first place banner?

It was decided to keep the chronology going and hang the banners up. All second place banners remained white, boys' championship banners (three) were gold, and the girls' (fourteen) were purple. What a distraction for opponents. When Dax's team won the championship in 2001, a new tradition started: we put up 3½ x 5 foot pictures of the winners on the wall. These were a distraction to hometown players and visitors alike.

Don't Let Success Go to Your Head

Sportswriter Grantland Rice wrote, "Failure isn't so bad if it doesn't attack the heart. Success is all right if it doesn't go to the head."[1] A repeat championship carries with it the opportunity to gloat and "let it go to your head." We needed to keep failures and successes alike in perspective and not personalize either too much.

Dax's senior season was full of emotion and distractions. The boys were now in the spotlight with the girls and expected to do well this year. The two previous years the team was ranked sixth and seventh going into the state tournaments. We were not expected to beat the bigger and better teams around the state. This year was not the same. Every team we played knew who we were and wanted a "piece" of us. New strategies, offenses, and defenses came at us in every game. Many games were rough and tumble, crowds were raucous and rowdy. Opposing cheerleaders were much bolder and wanted us to know exactly how we were going to lose. Visiting crowds to our gym were angrier.

One of the most interesting strategies to beat us was used in a game when we overheard the opposing coach giving instruction to one of his players to "stay on Dax's left for the next two hours." He was to "concentrate on guarding Dax's left side since Dax obviously had no right, and this would take away Dax's ability to play." This strategy was used the year before and had failed each time. However, this tenacious player followed his coach's instructions admirably.

During time outs he came to our huddle and stood next to Dax's left arm. There was a strange blue shirt in our huddle all night long, and we were dressed in our "light whites." When Dax came to the sideline during play to get instructions from Coach Scott, the tenacious blue jersey followed and listened to Coach Scott's instructions also. During half time when Dax stopped at the

> IN YOUR PATIENCE POSSESS YE YOUR SOULS.
>
> *Luke 21:19*

water fountain, a blue jersey stopped with him and when Dax turned the corner to enter our dressing room, a blue jersey followed him. To allow Coach Scott the opportunity to do his job, the assistant coaches blocked him from entering the dressing room. Undaunted, the young man stood as close as he could to the door and performed his duty the best he could. I complimented him on his attitude and determination and told him we would love to have him on our team. Finally, his own coach came around the corner and let the tenacious player go to his own dressing room.

Kirtland has three gymnasiums. The big gym, called "the Arena," is larger than most junior college gyms and can hold over 4,000 fans. Around the Navajo Reservation, however, this gym size is normal and even small compared to some 6,000-plus seat gyms. The crowds often chanted, "Yego Shash Yego!" ("Go, bears, go!"), and the traditional native drums thundered all night. Yego is a Navajo term of encouragement to do your best. In the smaller gyms it is absolutely deafening. We packed "houses" of all sizes that year. Good luck communicating with your players if you need to do something without calling a time-out. I am a quiet, stoic man, and I am more so when I coach. But I had to regularly throw down my clipboard with a thunderous clap to get the officials' attention to call a time-out. Beating the Kirtland Central Broncos was now every other team's goal.

THE BIG DANCE OR BUST

Our only losses that year came from Gallup High School and Farmington High School, our heated rival. In the first meeting, Dax took a "Clifton still charge" and was knocked unconscious by their six foot eight center. In the locker room, we asked him to start at one hundred and count down by seven. He got to ninety-three and hollered, "I wouldn't know the rest anyway." When he came out of the locker room, the crowd roared. He begged to get back in the game, but he went to the ER instead.

We met Farmington again in the district championship. We knew that it was not going to be an easy game to win, but our goal was not necessarily to win the district championship. I know this sounds strange to many, but our goal was always to go to the "big dance." Every year we drilled it into our players' heads that the big dance was the state championship and nothing else could take its place. A district championship was okay. The first place and the second place teams in the district go to the state tournament. We just had to be in the top two. When the district championships came around, we were physically in shape and ready. All our starters had returned from the previous year, except Derrick.

Every team was bigger than us, and Farmington was no exception. The newspapers predicted a loss for us again. We were indeed nervous and started off that way in the game. We missed several shots and had to climb out of a hole every quarter. It was the most physical game we played all year, but our tough schedule had prepared us. Players were shoving, slapping, and elbowing, and officials were not too liberal with whistles. We substituted players on and off the floor in an attempt to tire them out. They just knocked us down, and we were slow to get up. During time-outs we encouraged the boys to keep their focus and to remember what our ultimate goal was. We played our kind of basketball. Coach Scott tried to make his voice heard over the crowd, "Don't get into their style, and don't play like they're playing."

ALL-AMERICAN?

At halftime Coach Scott turned and said to me, "Wait here on the floor and accept an award for Dax." Coach Scott did not want to talk to the team at half with any of his players absent. I waited by the scorer's table, and a man started walking down the ramp. I had no idea who he was. He got to the scorer's table and asked for the microphone from our announcer. It was a wireless microphone, and he asked me to go to the middle of the court with him. At center court, he turned on the microphone and presented me with an award saying that Dax Crum was a member of the McDonald's All American team. I was dumbfounded. He then presented me with a book of coupons that Dax could use at local McDonald's restaurants. It was about a half a year's supply. As we walked off the floor, I asked him if this was a real award for a real All-American. He said, "Yes, we have been watching him for the last three years, since his sophomore performance against Albuquerque Academy, and he deserves this award." I put the plaque and coupons away and didn't tell Dax about them until after the game.

During the fourth quarter, we begged the officials to make calls so that the boys would not get hurt. Even Valerie, knowing the referees by name, weakly pleaded her boy's case. The pleas were ignored. Our opponents scored and were ahead of us. We brought the ball in from the far end of the court, and they put a full court press on us. The players were afraid of their combination of height and pressure, and it caused them to make too many mistakes. They did things they normally didn't do. They had practiced many times passing their way through the press, but this time Dax dribbled the ball toward Chase and gave it to him, and then Chase dribbled toward Devon and passed it to him. Devon then dribbled the ball down the floor just in front of our bench when, all of a sudden, he flew into our laps. Two opposing players ran a trap into him and swept him right off the floor. His eyes were full of frustration. Some of our fans, including Valerie, yelled at the referees and called them more than by name. Anger crept into our players. I grabbed Devon and said, "They won't get away with this in the Pit. Stay focused." He gave a perceptive smile, and I sensed he would keep his head on straight.

The team had a huddle. We went down the floor, scored

again, and kept the game close. Our opponents worked the ball around well on their next possession and scored again. When we brought the ball in, the opposing crowd behind me began to chant something different. I couldn't tell exactly what it was. I heard two syllables and nothing else, but I fixed my attention on that section of the crowd. What was it? We missed our next shot and we were falling behind. Was their chant working? What was it?

Our rivals came down the floor and scored again, and the new basket added fuel to the raging fire in the stands. This time I noticed that the new chant was employed only when Dax touched the ball. The chant rose right behind me in the stands. It sounded like "careful." Each time Dax touched the ball, the fanatics shouted louder. One of my players leaned over and asked, "Coach, do you hear what they're saying?" He moved closer and said the word—*cripple*. The chant was "Crip-ple, crip-ple, crip-ple." I never turned around to face down the crowd. They were probably unaware that I was the "cripple's" father. If I had reacted, it would have been more fuel for their arrogant fire. The crowd wanted a reaction to see if the taunt was effective.

The taunt *was* effective, but only in one way. I looked across the gym, knowing exactly where Valerie sat every game—the 4th row. She never brought her purse to ball games and therefore had no tissues. I noticed her high cheekbones were glistening, and with her long pretty fingers, she tried to keep the tears from showing.

We lost the game. The players lined up on the floor and congratulated each other on a well-played game. We would be playing the hard side of the bracket in the state tournament. On the way to the locker room, our fans asked me if I had heard what the opposing crowd had been chanting. I said, "Of course." They asked me what I planned to do about it. I said, "Nothing."

When we got to the locker room, I asked Dax if he had heard what was being chanted, and he told me that he hadn't discerned any of their words. I said, "Good." He said, "Why?" I said, "Oh, it was nothing. Never mind."

The jeering was meaningless because he gave them no heed. I was actually glad that we had lost the game because of physical play rather than verbal bashing. We kept our eyes on the prize—the big dance. We could have played much more aggressively with the result of players hurt and missing the state tournament.

Several people approached me the following week and asked what I planned to do about the cripple chant.

"Coach, don't let them get away with that."

"Coach, are you going to sue them?"

Who would I sue? What would be the complaint? Several people brought it up at the next school board meeting, but they were talking to the wrong school board. They should have gone down the street to the next town's school board meeting. The cripple chant was the talk of the community for a couple of weeks, but it soon fizzled out.

The first game of the playoffs put us in Las Cruces at Onate High School again. It was a very close game, and we never could put them away. It was a wake-up call for us. We went into the Pit much wiser. Back in the Lobos dressing room, we got ready for Roswell, our next opponent. No, their mascot is not an alien, although Dax thought "that would be sweet."

Dax played the best game of his high school career. He finished the game with twenty-five points and ten assists. He was unstoppable. I noticed some college coaches up in the rafters taking some real notice. They frantically wrote notes, took stats, and made calls back to their head coaches. The final score was 86–63.

LEGITIMATE PLAYER!

We were fortunate to meet Farmington for one last show-down in the final state championship game. The announcer introduced our rivals, and they went to the far free throw line. They watched us as we were introduced. When the starters walked to the TV cameras to be introduced, I leaned over to Dax and talked about the opponents, briefly discussing the opponents' body language. I was a communications minor in college, so I told him who had aggressive stances and who showed signs of fear. I told Dax, "Attack him, him, and him. They are scared to death." He did just that. As a result, the game was not even close.

It was the most boring of all the championships. We led by twenty-five points in the fourth quarter. We took their crowd out of the game because we again "heeded them not." Of the 15,000 people, most went home disappointed, but the few Kirtland fans left redeemed. We played with team-work and discipline. We were unselfish and kept focus—final score: 67–52. All of our team received playing time. The state newspapers ran articles saying, "Crum Proves Himself Again." It was a far cry from two years earlier when the headlines read, "Legitimate Player?"

Dax finished his high school career starting in the North-South All-Star Game. New Mexico is divided in half, and for this game the northern players play the southern players. He was the only 4A starter in the game. All the other starters for both teams were from 5A schools. In the words of Pistol Pete, Dax "put on a show." The crowd rose to their feet with each backspin or behind the back move. Playing against the best in the state, he scored sixteen points, 6 of 9 shooting from the field and 2 of 3 from the foul line—hardly the work of a boy who some called a "cripple." His teammates and the crowd gave him a standing ovation for his last win in the Pit. That year Dax was named first team

All-state, New Mexico North-South All-Star game starter, McDonald's All-American, and "cripple." Then, as now, he didn't want to be called any of these titles or names. Life is filled with ironies. Titles and names—good or bad—mean little to him. He focuses on being his best and seldom heeds the world.

If you enter the Kirtland arena today, you will see three huge pictures of the three-peat state championships on the wall above your head. These young men absolutely gave the proverbial 110 percent in order to win those victories.

Chapter 14

SCHOLARSHIP

Dax finished his senior year competing in track and field. His favorite event was the 110 meter high hurdles. He would get up early to run hurdles before school to give himself an edge. He was ranked at the top of the state with a time of fifteen seconds flat. The state track meet was coming up, and he was the favored winner. One day, he came home after practice in agony. We met at the door.

He complained, "My back is killing me."

I didn't respond immediately. Finally, I sputtered, "Get in the truck. We gotta go." He was confused but hopped in the passenger's seat. We didn't speak until Dax noticed where we were going. We stopped in front of the Farmington Hospital.

Dax said, "Dad, I'm not hurting that bad."

I answered, "We're not here for you."

We were there to take Val home. After having a doctor's appointment, Valerie had been admitted to the hospital, where we learned the reason for Valerie's chronic fatigue: renal cancer. She had a softball size tumor in her kidney, and the whole kidney needed to be removed as soon as possible. The surgeon was the parent of a Farmington High basketball player. I liked him; he was a good doctor. Dax was immaturely skeptical but got over it soon. The surgeon didn't have any grudges, and the surgery was a success. Valerie responded positively, and it seemed we were in the clear.

Val was feeling good enough to be released from the hospital, but later that night Dax was checked in. His back pain grew worse and moved to his lungs, which were wearing down from pneumonia. That night Dax did not sleep. Instead, he coughed so much that blood finally appeared. Then came the nonstop vomiting. Valerie walked into the bathroom to see Dax on his knees, his head hanging over the toilet. She packed him up and headed back to the hospital. Dax stayed a week, missing the state track meet. He did not intend to end his high school sports career in this way.

Unfortunately for us, Val's cancer had metastasized to her lungs, liver, and bones. She valiantly stuck to her cancer regimen, but the effects were still present and worsening. Money to support her cancer treatments dwindled. Anyone who has experienced paying for cancer treatments knows, even with insurance, how much money can be spent on pills, medicines, treatments, and travel expenses. Dax was willing to take a scholarship in any sport and work as hard as he could to help out.

Coach Scott sent out some tapes of Dax's basketball games to a lot of colleges. Responses were positive, especially when they saw Dax's stats and how he helped his team win three straight state championships. We visited a few local schools, Division II schools. Dax scrimmaged with their teams, but college basketball coaches couldn't seem to get past the one-handedness. I guess they needed to sit a little further down in the Pit.

We talked to schools about soccer. Dax made his own tapes and sent out numerous copies. In return, he got a handful of letters and even received a call from the Princeton soccer coach, but the Ivy League school didn't give athletic scholarships. The offers were weak even with his being the New Mexico soccer scoring champion for two years in a row. I expected calls from UCLA or UCONN. Finally we got decent offers from two junior college schools in Arizona.

WHEREVER YOU GO, GO WITH ALL YOUR HEART.

Confucius

Yavapai College was the perennial soccer champs for the NJCAA (National Junior College Athletic Association). They wanted Dax for soccer, but the funds would not be available until his second year with the program. They wanted him to prove himself in his first year. I felt like saying to the many colleges "you're missing out." The only other "real" offer came from Arizona Western College, a two-year school, but we got what we had prayed for—a full scholarship. It would keep him going to school for two years, and we didn't need to worry about his ability to receive an education. I didn't have to decide whether to spend money on cancer treatments or college textbooks.

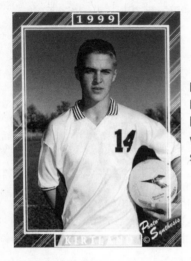

Dax was a great soccer player. He later played soccer and basketball in college. Dax was a two time New Mexico state scoring leader.

Dax with three of the seniors that he played with during his sophomore year. Left to right, Dax, Clifton, Zach, and Kenny.

Coach Steve Scott directs traffic in the tough St. Pius gym, including Dax, (#10).

Dax scoring two of his 14 points against Albuquerque Academy in the state championship game, 2001

Derrick Woody (45), Dax (10), and Chase Hathaway (20) get ready to play defense against Artesia, NM. Dax shot a perfect 9 for 9 from the floor against Artesia.

Dax (6'2"), surrounded by Chargers and 15,000 fans, elevates high enough to shoot over 6'5" Albuquerque Academy center during the 2001 championship game.

The Daily Times

Richard and Dax Crum exult at the repeat championship against Las Cruces Onate.

Dax in championship shooting form against Roswell, New Mexico. He finished with 25 points and 10 assists.

Father and son photo taken at the Bronco at the San Juan County Fairgrounds, New Mexico.

Three-peat champion varsity starter three years in a row.

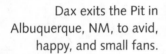

Dax exits the Pit in Albuquerque, NM, to avid, happy, and small fans.

Dax and parents before the NM All-star game in Albuquerque. The only 4A boy to start the game. Could Dax compete against 5A All-stars?

Dax competing in the high hurdles (in correct uniform).

Dax—one-handed, not one-armed—driving in for two against Phoenix South Mountain Community College. Give every opportunity maximum effort.

6'2" Dax flying through Yavapai College timber with his 6'10" teammate trailing on the fast break. (Notice the size of Dax's hand on the ball.)

Dax's AWC soccer scholarship was secure, but could he walk on to a top-notch basketball program at the same time?

Chapter 15

IF YOU CAN'T STAND THE HEAT, STAY OUT OF YUMA

After accepting the only scholarship offer, Dax loaded up his little red truck and drove to Yuma, Arizona, where the temperatures reach 115 degrees. How could anybody play soccer in this environment? Where was the indoor, air-conditioned stadium that would protect the players from heat exhaustion and heat stroke? That was too expensive. They just split up the 90-minute game into four quarters with mandatory water breaks.

Dax's team practiced at seven in the morning and seven at night in order to offset the punishing sun. Even at night the temperature was still over 105, and the players took precautions to stay hydrated. None of the players wore shin guards or high socks because the more you wore, the slower you became. The more they played, the more sweat-drenched their jerseys became. When they chose sides for a scrimmage, every player wanted to be a "skin." If a player wasn't a skin, his jersey became so soaked with perspiration he started moving slower and slower. I told Dax to keep his shirt on because the extra weight of his soaked clothes would toughen up his legs.

YUMA WILDLIFE

At the night practices, the wildlife in Yuma came out of their natural shady shelters, and the players frequently ran around bullfrogs, snakes, and tall, ugly jackrabbits. The Canadian players called the jackrabbits "bandidos." They

---

ACT WELL THY PART

Shakespeare

---

looked like German shepherds bounding across the field. After one evening practice, a big snake worked its way out into the middle of the field,

looking for a tiny bandido or toad. All the players refused to run their sprints. Coach Fermanis, the soccer coach, yelled, "Just run around it!" The players were exhausted and each gladly waited for a manager to shoo the six-foot-long bull snake to the sidelines, where he could head to better hunting grounds in the lettuce fields.

During August and September, Dax had grueling two-a-day practices with six-mile runs. The heat never really broke until about the end of September. During this time he started to play pickup games in basketball in order to "stay in basketball shape."

DON'T "WALK ON"—RUN ON

When October came, it was time to make a huge decision. Would he go after his first love (basketball) or stay secure with a sure full-ride soccer scholarship? Basketball tryouts were starting, and Dax was confident he could make the team. In the team scrimmages, he did more than his fair share of "schooling." Coach Fermanis was concerned that soccer would not be first priority for Dax, but he did not object to Dax trying out for the basketball team. Could Dax do it though? Fermanis worried about the physical toll that permanent two-a-days would have on Dax. Would Coach

Green even allow him to try out?

Coach Kelly Green had already received a video tape from Coach Scott at Kirtland Central High School showing Dax playing in the state championships. The games were filmed from the top of the Pit, and like I said, it was hard to notice Dax was missing a hand. Coach Green wasn't impressed enough to offer a scholarship, but when Dax called Coach Green, he welcomed him to try out and become a member of the team as a walk-on. Later, Coach Green walked into the athletic office and noticed that Dax had already been offered a full soccer scholarship. Green and Fermanis met in the office and Fermanis said, "You realize he only has one hand, don't you?" Coach Green replied, "C'mon, that's not true. I've seen him on video tape."

Dax was ready to try out for the basketball team. Green ran the team through very rigorous defensive close-out drills. He was testing the players to get to a spot on the floor without getting beaten. It was a drill directed at the hearts of the players; fortunately, Dax's heart had been tested many times. The next test put the players on teams, and they played several games. Dax still felt that Coach Green wanted to see how much "fight" the players had in them. Which player would quit first? All the players had offensive skills, but who would still play defense? Who was going to quit on him? Defense is a good test for determining who has heart because most players in high school and college like to coast on defense. Dax began to see a niche where he could definitely be an asset to this team.

PAYOFF

Dax's persistence paid off after one week. He walked into the gym each day and asked an assistant coach if they had chosen the team yet. Each day was the same, but after only one week, he had impressed the coaches enough to get the nod. His name was posted as a collegiate basketball player. The Arizona Western Matadors now had another full-time basketball player and a full-time soccer player. It was a case of two athletes for the price of one.

I knew that Dax wanted to make the team so that he could show the cynics that a one-handed boy could make a college basketball team. I also knew that he would never be happy sitting on the bench. The coaches wanted to redshirt Dax his first year to give him experience. He said, "I'll think about it."

He called home that night and asked Valerie and me what to do. Should he try to play this year or sit it out as a redshirt? Valerie made up both our minds. She took the phone.

"You tell your coach you want to play!"

"Yes, ma'am."

During this time Dax had an ally/spy in Professor Hawkey. She taught family studies, and Dax enjoyed her class. She checked on Dax's progress by frequently asking the coaches, "How is Dax doing? Is he going the make the team? Is he going to travel with the team? Do you think he'll play?" Each time she inquired, his status improved.

Dax didn't see much basketball playing time and mainly supported the team with defensive efforts during practice. Many would call his team the "dummy squad." He was a passionate player and cheered his team on. He would sit at the end of the bench during games and was the first to congratulate and encourage. This was where Dax's collection of quotes came into use again. Now he put into practice Shakespeare's quote, "What e'er thou art, act well thy part." He knew what "part" to play. It was different from the part he played in high school. He was the positive reinforcement, so he played the part and continues to play the part. When teammates came off the floor, they received plenty of high fives or a "high one."

He was exhausted every night. Luckily two-a-days for soccer were over, but practices for basketball and soccer continued. He went to school from 8:00 a.m. to 2:00 p.m. in order to keep up with a sixteen credit hour schedule. Dax knew that school came first, and he took advantage of the full scholarship. He then headed to basketball, which got out at 5:00 p.m. He hurried to the cafeteria to eat quickly and then went to soccer practice at 7:00 p.m. When soccer was done, he slowly walked to the dorm. Some football players begged him to keep his body odor at a distance. His jersey was often soaked, and his body was sore from trying to box out six-foot-ten basketball players for two hours and then chase five-foot-eight soccer players for another two hours. A shower was a piece of heaven if he stayed awake long enough to untie his shoes.

> THERE IS NO SUBSTITUTE FOR HARD WORK.
>
> *Thomas A. Edison*

FAMILY FIRST

Valerie's health was not improving despite the treatments, some even in Mexico. She had missed soccer season, and basketball games were just beginning. It was time to watch her boy play. Valerie's older sister, Sue, wanted to take us to San Diego for the next cancer treatment, and Yuma was on our way. Our Christmas vacation was spent fighting cancer. It was going to be a quick trip, but maybe she could see her boy in a college game. When we arrived at the center, it was closed for the holiday, and Valerie was distraught. She was practicing being positive, but she couldn't get her treatment. Valerie found it so discouraging, and tears seemed to help a little. It was a good time for a big sister to be near, and Sue quickly offered a solution. Everything worked out. I took the bus across Arizona, and Dax's older brother Baric picked me up in New Mexico. Valerie stayed until the center opened up. She then got her treatment and also saw one of Dax's games.

SERVICE TO GOD AND COUNTRY

Valerie and I have a strong tradition of service to God and country. Service was desired and expected. Dax was approaching the age that would be ideal to serve as a missionary. I had told him many times that when the time came, everything else could be put on hold, and life would resume later. Dax was ready and willing to go.

Shaking hands is a common greeting, especially in the southwest. Shaking hands with Dax is, in his words, "Really weird." He gets all types of handshakes. He has even named some of them. One of the most common is the "mystery shake." People grab ahold of Dax's wrist and begin sliding their hand up and down his arm until they find a frightening stump. The next is the "baby bird." People shake with two hands until they cup his little hand, bringing it closer to their faces with a tender, "Aww, poor thing," like it had just fallen from the nest. Last, and Dax's favorite, is the "double shake." This handshake involves a quick squeeze and immediate release as the person's eyes meet Dax's uncomfortably. With eyes wide, he or she quickly reattach the grasp.

I wondered if shaking hands would be different if he were dressed as a missionary. Financially, family and friends were more than willing to help us pay Dax's way, wherever he went. I scheduled a meeting with our bishop, the spiritual leader over our congregation, and we discussed the future. He had been to our home numerous times to check on us and comfort Valerie. I was direct. I said, "Bishop, I need to know if Dax needs to serve a mission now." The bishop was a large man. He looked me in the eye and said, "Dax is where he needs to be. He is touching the hearts of many people." Dax

> BE UNSELFISH. THAT IS THE FIRST AND FINAL COMMANDMENT FOR THOSE WHO WOULD BE USEFUL AND HAPPY IN THEIR USEFULNESS.
>
> *Charles William Eliot*

had become very good friends with his ward's bishop, Bishop Hawkey, the spouse of his family studies professor and advocate with the basketball coaches. I had the same conversation with him. He also assured me that Dax was where he needed to be. That became evident in the forthcoming days.

Dax was touching people's hearts, even from the bench. He hadn't received any playing time thus far, and there was no reason to expect that he would play in the next two games, either. A junior college from Milwaukee, Wisconsin, flew into Yuma. They were scheduled for back-to-back games for the next two days. Valerie came alone to the first game, but Dax never left the bench because the game was too close for Coach Green to put Dax in for charity minutes. It was a very close game, and the Matadors won. The second night of the double header, Dax's teammates stepped it up, and Coach Green knew that Dax's mom was in town to see him play. When the Matadors pushed their lead to twenty, Coach Green put Dax in the game, his first college basketball game. Dax knew that this was his chance.

First and Lasting Impressions

With only two minutes to play, Dax had to impress his coaches. What can be done in two minutes? Dax had never been afraid of fouling an opponent. To him, a foul was simply the by-product of great hustle. Maximum effort comes with increased momentum and contact. But how long does it take for a heart to be touched? How long would it take to change a coach's mind? Dax entered the game, and people started to point and clap when they saw that a one-handed player had walked

> **KEEP YOUR FACE TO THE SUNSHINE AND YOU CANNOT SEE THE SHADOW.**
>
> *Helen Keller*

onto the floor. The fans at AWC (Arizona Western College) in Yuma are 90 percent gray haired and come from all over the country to enjoy the dry, paradisiacal, winter weather. The small gym erupted for the physically challenged player. When the game was over, Dax came away with two fouls, two steals, and six points.

Valerie yelled with all her energy for her son. It was the last time she got after a referee for making the wrong call on her boy. It was the last time she cheered him on to victory. Her baby was now a college basketball player, which many said would never happen, but she knew better. Dax thanked Coach Green for the once in a lifetime opportunity.

That night, Dax and his mother ate authentic Mexican tacos from the Jack's Taco Stand to celebrate his college debut and later watched classic movies. They cherished the milestone moment. They talked, laughed, and cried until she left for her last treatment.

What Else Does It Take?

Several times during the season, the team held shooting contests with all the players. Dax won all but one of the contests. I knew Dax had great confidence in his shooting, but it still wasn't enough for the college-level coaches. One month later, Dax mentioned to his coach that he wanted to play Division I basketball. Dax knew that this inquiry would be met with skepticism, but he persisted anyway. Coach Green told Dax that in order to play Division I ball, a player had to be exceptional at one particular skill. Dax knew he had to find a way.

During the season Dax wondered what he could do to get more playing time. How could he be a better asset to the team so that playing time came easier and quicker? How could he impress the coaches to the point that they would take a chance on a one-handed player? Should he be the first one on the floor every day? Should he practice harder than any other player? Should he stay longer than the other players every day? He did all these things, but nothing seemed to work.

Chapter 16

FIND A WAY

Maximum hustle, superior shooting, early arrivals, late stays, and being a "team player" had increased Dax's playing time, but perhaps great defensive skills would take his game to the next level. Dax focused on ways to improve his defensive skills, whereas most basketball players focus and work hard on offense. And that's how Dax discovered his opportunity. Even though he was already the best shooter on the team, he was determined to daily improve defensively to be ready with superior guarding and stopping efforts when those great dribbling and shooting opponents stepped onto the floor. Most players wanted their name in the newspaper, and the way to do that was to get points. With Dax, though, he just wanted to play, and defense would get him onto the floor.

The first season of soccer produced an even win-loss record, with Dax as the leading scorer. Dax rarely left the field. In his first year at Yuma in basketball, the team won twenty-two and lost nine games. Before his second semester was over, Dax left early because his mother's condition had become worse, and there wasn't much time left. His teachers were contacted, and they helped Dax finish his schoolwork so he could get home.

HELL IS TRUTH SEEN TOO LATE—DUTY NEGLECTED IN ITS SEASON.

Tryon Edwards

Dax made it home to see his mother in her debilitated condition. As Valerie lay in her last moments, she pulled each of her children close one at a time and whispered to them. When Dax's turn came, she pulled him close and whispered, "My hero—choose the right." Those were her last words to him. Everyone in the room knew it was time for her to go.

Her passing was tough—tougher than any basketball or soccer hecklers. With them, Dax had time—time to change their minds, time to work on getting better. With his mother, time had run out. Dax confided in me why her passing was so hard: "Teenagers think they know it all."

Dax wrote "Hell is truth seen too late—duty neglected in its season" on the board for his team to read before his next basketball game. It was one of the most important lessons Dax learned in his life, but like most lessons it was learned after the fact. The truth was he, like most of us, took his mom for granted. He didn't have a chance to thank her for all she did, for washing his soccer socks and getting them so white, for cooking the pregame meals to perfection, for always believing in him, and for teaching him to live honorably. He wanted to say sorry, sorry for coming home late after curfew, for not finishing his pig chores, and for not taking the time to say, "I love you!" time and again.

During the funeral, we sat together, and I watched him review the events of his life just as he had done on the way home from basketball camp. He asked himself what he was supposed to do now. The solution did not come easily or soon. We both grieved at her passing like we had never grieved in this life.

We spent the next few months learning to do our own cooking and cleaning. I wondered how I would take care of Dax's two teenage sisters, McKenzie and Afton. They were fondly nicknamed "the little girls," only they weren't so little anymore.

FINDING THE WAY BACK

Then, the next school year was starting and Dax's soccer coach desperately wanted to know if his leading scorer was returning. I told Dax he needed to go back to Yuma. He did, fully equipped with a new skill—his mother's selflessness. He now looked at others first. What their goals were, their feelings. He had a new duty and a new season, and he was not going to neglect it.

The second year was even harder than the first. Why? Because he was already a member of both basketball and soccer teams when he showed up, and two-a-days were in progress for both sports. Just because soccer was first in the year didn't mean basketball could be put off. Most of the basketball players were returning players for their second year, and they expected a greater commitment from each other. Their 22–9 record was a disappointment. They wanted to win more.

Dax's commitment overflowed into his academic schedule also. The first semester he signed up for twenty-two "insane" credit hours, but in the second semester he was easy on himself and took only twenty-one credit hours. Most serious scholarship athletes sign up for only twelve to fifteen hours. Dax wanted to get the most out of his scholarship and try for two associate degrees at once.

> THE BUSY HAVE NO TIME FOR TEARS
>
> *Lord Byron*

Once again, basketball practices were in the afternoon, followed by soccer practices at 7:00 p.m. Dax excelled in the soccer conference as the runner-up in the scoring race for the Arizona Community College league. Dax also stepped up his commitment to church activities and took a couple of football and basketball players to church with him. Most of the students usually did nothing on Sundays or headed to Mexico for the weekends. One friend told Dax during a church meeting that a lot of the girls at AWC wanted to get married but not until after they were through partying.

Although soccer season had a better win-loss record, the basketball season was just terrific. The team lost only one conference game and was ranked number one in the country. I was able to catch several games that year, and I began to see a lady in Mesa, Arizona, who had also lost her spouse to cancer. Her name was Kristi, and she later became my second wife. When we were married, the basketball season was in full swing, so I was in town to see all the games in the valley. Dax's tenacity impressed the coaches and his playing time increased to where he was considered the sixth man (first substitute) on the team. A player fatigued—send in Dax. A teammate got in foul trouble—send in Dax.

The basketball team stepped it up and went to nationals. Coach Green hit upon a great strategy. He would wait until a few minutes had passed and then he would send two defensive players onto the floor. Dax, nicknamed "the Legend," and another player, nicknamed "the Rocket," would enter the games as sixth and seventh players to provide full court pressure. The competition was demoralized to have such aggressive defensive players guarding them so tightly, especially at the end of a game. The team finished the season with a 31-3 record.

Dax played a significant amount of minutes for a team that was extremely successful. His best game was probably against Glendale Community College in the west Phoenix area. AWC's best player was ejected from the game on a quirky play, and that opened the door for Dax to play more.

> MY FATHER GAVE ME THE GREATEST GIFT ANYONE COULD GIVE ANOTHER PERSON—HE BELIEVED IN ME.
>
> *Jim Valvano*

One of the local newspapers caught the game and wrote, "Dax Crum produced his second straight good game. The sophomore scored 17 points, including 4 three-pointers." The game was won with a score of 96-69.

During that season Dax called to let me know he was nominated for the "Jimmy V. Comeback Award." He asked, "Who is Jimmy V., and what did he come back from?" I informed him of the North Carolina State list of accomplishments, including winning the NCAA championship on the Pit where Dax had won of his high school championships. It ended with Jimmy's battle with cancer. Dax didn't know who nominated him, but he was honored, even though the award went to another student at the University of Texas. Dax listened to Jim Valano's last big speech that he gave at the ESPY Awards:

> To me, there are three things we all should do every day. We should do this every day of our lives. Number one is laugh. You should laugh every day. Number two is think. You should spend some time in thought. And number three is, you should have your emotions moved to tears. It could be happiness or joy. But think about it. If you laugh, you think, and you cry, that's a full day. That's a heck of a day. You do that seven days a week, you're going to have something special.[1]

Dax loves this quote. Laugh every day, think or ponder

about your life, and invest enough feelings in what you do to be moved to tears—this is greatness. Sometimes it's hard for people who haven't experienced cancer to appreciate what this means.

Dax's team finished the National Junior College Athletic Association sweet sixteen. Six sophomores received Division I offers, but Dax came up empty-handed once again.

Chapter 17

D-1 OR NOT D-1

Awaiting his third year of college, Dax received real soccer offers from Irvine, California, and Dayton, Ohio. Dax was a great soccer player who had been tested repeatedly. However, soccer was not his first love. Basketball and soccer are amazingly similar sports, but to Dax basketball was more intense and fun. Basketball has action that is more concentrated than soccer. Dax often said, "Every trip down the floor, I can do something to help my team win." With soccer, a player often did not touch the ball for ten minutes at a time. Basketball seemed more challenging, which heightened his eagerness and provided a chance to prove himself.

Each level of competition has a standard of expectation. If you were a successful high school athlete, you know the level it takes to participate in high school. But this is where the "feels good" participation in sports ends. Junior college athletes know competition is dramatically increased over the high school level. NCAA Division I basketball is the most competitive level of amateur basketball. Division I coaches and programs are under pressure from serious administrators and unforgiving media to win. In fact, it often comes down to "win this season or it will be your last." Picking up a kid

> I DON'T THINK HUMAN BEINGS LEARN ANYTHING WITHOUT DESPERATION.
>
> *Jim Carrey*

who's not going to seriously add to the program's winning chance is not a thought D-I coaches will dare entertain. Competing at the highest level would not be easy for Dax, but he felt it was his calling. His life's mission was to play D-I basketball.

His teammates at AWC encouraged him. After all, they knew how good Dax was and what he was capable of doing on the basketball floor. What was harder for Dax was the pessimism that he heard constantly, even from close friends and family: "Why don't you just get a job? Are you still trying for this Division I thing? You have done all right with your situation."

Dax had grown weary of the pity, the patronization, or the outright disbelief. Dax called around, inquired into programs, and made several road trips. He even headed to the BYU and University of Utah area. He called coaches on the phone. He scrimmaged anywhere they'd let him, but the coaches never talked to him or returned his calls. He was disappointed and started back for Arizona. He stopped in Cedar City, a small town in southern Utah, to help his older brother Justin move his family. Cedar City is known mainly for its Shakespearean festivals and outdoor fun, but it also has a college. Before they finished packing, Justin offered to take Dax down to Southern Utah University (SUU) to meet the head coach. In the car Dax asked Justin, "Is Southern Utah University a Division I school?"

The assistant coach at SUU was Coach Carillo, who had been to the National Junior College finals and had seen Dax play on many other occasions. He reported to Coach Evans, the head coach, about different players. So Coach Evans met Dax and knew who Dax was. He offered Dax an opportunity to make the team as a walk on, but there would be no money. Coach Evans then instructed Dax that if he made the team, he was not to be a "cancer." Dax said, "Yes, sir," knowing he could make it and did so with ease.

Coach Evans was surprised with Dax's basketball skills, but he had already recruited his scorers, so he advised Dax to be a team player. Dax always had a scorer's mentality, but that mentality needed to be suppressed for the good of the team and the coaches. He was to be more analytical about the game in specific areas in order to help the team.

This was where he developed his "basketball mind." He searched game DVDs for an edge against opponents. Game strategies, player analyses, and studying winning techniques were daily tasks. He studied games, teammates' tendencies, and why certain moves worked for certain players and not for others. In his younger years, dribbling and shooting was the focus. It was now a disciplined race to secure a mental edge. Dax cheered for his team at the end of the bench and watched his team lose again and again. Coach Evans grew more and more frustrated with his scorers.

Assistant Coach Carrillo usually ran the substitutes into the games. During the game against Western Illinois, his desperation climaxed to the point that he finally considered Dax for play during the first—not the usual second—half. This was Dax's dream come true, even if he was the coach's last resort. At last, Dax would be a Division I college basketball player.

He entered the game with a lot of confidence. The first time down the floor,

IF WE REMAIN HUMBLE AND HUNGRY, WE CAN WIN.

Dave Allison

Illinois's best guard looked arrogantly at Dax. Dax's excitement of finally being on the floor was replaced with panic. The seasoned opponent gave Dax a quick jab step and a head fake, and he left Dax in his dust—two point layup. "Schooled!" Dax's anger kicked in, and the next time down the floor, he was determined to keep the ball out of the hands of their top gun. He employed a tight defense so that the star guard couldn't keep up his scoring binge. The guard sprinted around the key and then went to the baseline. He hesitated and tried to rub Dax off on a big player who was setting a screen. Dax and the big screener collided shoulders, and Dax's shoulder lost. His body absorbed the impact, and his shoulder separated, which was attached to his "good" arm that he used to dress with, eat with, and bathe with. His left arm hung limply, and he knew something was seriously wrong because of the excruciating pain. Dax later learned that he would be out a minimum of six weeks. Dax had done it, had been an official D-I player for one minute and thirteen seconds, but it was stolen away by an injury. It was over before he could really get started.

During his injury, Dax petitioned his apartment neighbors for help, especially when he had to get dressed. He had to do everything one handed, and that hand was attached to a bum shoulder. The next game was a gimme game against a Division II school. He had his shoulder injected with some local anesthetic so he at least could play without feeling the pain. With some painful twists of the needle that dropped down into the joint space, the burning fluid was slowly pushed in. The shoulder space was so tight it felt like a balloon was being blown up with every push of the syringe, but the pain disappeared. The doctor said it would bring four hours of relief—enough time to play a full basketball game. Dax was excited. Warming up he felt great. Then tiny stabs of pain hit his good arm, and after twenty minutes, the pain was full blown again. Dax begged the doctor and trainer for more injections, but the doctor said no. There was too much risk of long-term damage to Dax's more functional arm.

COACH AND BE COACHED!

During practices, Dax watched enthusiastically, but when game time arrived he was deeply discouraged. Game after game, the head athletic trainer, Ricky, did an ultrasound on Dax's arm, gave electronic stimulation to his muscles, and then taped bags of ice to Dax's body with plastic wrap.

Ricky was a big fan of Dax. He had heard of Dax's great soccer career at Arizona Western College, and they talked a lot about basketball and soccer. Before one basketball game, Ricky had started Dax's treatment when a starter on the team needed Ricky's attention. So he called Ashley, a student athletic trainer, to finish the ultrasound. Ashley was already a gifted athletic trainer and captain of the SUU women's soccer team. Ricky told her, "Dax is a soccer player too. He was a great scorer down in his conference in Arizona." Already impressed by the one-handed basketball player, Ashley was even more interested in the two-footed soccer player.

The season ended with SUU Thunderbirds losing in the first round of the conference tournament. Dax was off the "disabled list," but he never got off the bench. It was SUU's typical end to its basketball season. The coaches held exit interviews with all the players to finish out the school year. Dax had plenty of questions but settled

> A REJECTION IS NOTHING MORE THAN A NECESSARY STEP IN THE PURSUIT OF SUCCESS.
>
> *Bo Bennett*

> ## TOUGH TIMES NEVER LAST, BUT TOUGH PEOPLE DO.
>
> *Robert H. Schuller*

on asking only one, a constructive question that would help him improve: "What do I need to do or work on to be able to play?"

Coach Evans and Coach Carillo called Dax into their office together. Dax was glad that Coach Carillo was there because he felt that Coach Carillo liked him, and he had often determined who played in the games. Dax asked the question, eager to receive advice to better himself. Instead, the coaches asked Dax a simple question in return: "At this level of basketball you have to pass and dribble for extended periods with your right hand. Can you do that?" Dax couldn't believe it—this was his constructive feedback! He couldn't really answer yes, so he looked down at the floor and said, "No, I'm sorry."

He called me afterwards and recited the conversation word for word. It was discouraging news, and Dax's heart was broken. The thought of arguing with them was distasteful, and he despised begging. He left the office with even more questions running through his mind. Should I even try to come back? Should I quit? Why had they put me in there to guard Western Illinois's top player? Did they want me to be humiliated in front of thousands of fans? Is this a pity party for a handicapped kid? Am I fooling myself? When I practice every day, am I really helping the team? Do I really have the skill to compete at this level? Realistically, the coaches were telling Dax that he could be on the team but couldn't play because he had no right hand.

Chapter 18

ASHLEY

Dax got a summer job washing windows to save money for whatever the future held for him. He stayed in shape physically by running around campus and sneaking into the PE building to shoot. One Sunday, Dax made a comedic remark in Sunday school. Ashley, the athletic trainer that had helped Dax recuperate, laughed and came up to him after the meeting. She remembered how the head trainer Ricky had told her that Dax was a great soccer player. She asked Dax if he would participate in the Utah Summer Games and be on her three-on-three soccer team. He said, "I need some practice."

The tournament was the following weekend. Ashley called Dax to practice with her and a group of their friends. For Ashley, the practice was more of a tryout. She wanted to see if Dax was indeed good enough to play for their team, eloquently named "Freakin' Awesome." They met at the soccer field and chose teams. Ashley was on the same team as him. She gave him a quick through pass, and Dax split the two opposing defenders for a fantastic goal. Four more goals followed, and Ashley stopped the practice, smiled at Dax, and said, "Okay! You made the team."

The first game of the tournament arrived on Friday

WHERE ONE DOOR SHUTS ANOTHER OPENS.

Cervantes

evening. Ashley's friends sat next to Dax and quizzed him about his dating status and hinted that Ashley's status was single too. "Freakin' Awesome" won the game handily, with Dax scoring a hat trick. The two soccer stars walked slowly back to Dax's old, red truck. Ashley threw every hint she could.

"Are you doing anything tonight?" she asked. Dax responded without hesitation, "No, you wanna do something?" Although he said it like it was his idea, Ashley knew she had done the work. Dax suggested dinner.

Dax ordered steak, wanting to impress her with his refined cutting techniques. After he finished cutting, he looked at her and could tell she was not impressed. Instead, she reached across the table and stabbed a perfect one-inch cube of oozing red meat. "That's how we eat in my family!" she said. Dax repaid the favor by stealing a piece of Alfredo chicken.

Most young people don't consider whether the people around them are good, mediocre, or excellent-minded. But chances for success are enhanced by surrounding yourself with great people who have ambition and passion. A popular thought says that we should accept people for who they are. We try so hard to not judge others, but we really should judge others by judging correctly. We should not categorize without knowing what is really inside them. Confucius said it best: "I want you to be everything that's you deep in the center of your being." Dax and Ashley started learning what the other wanted. They each wanted to accomplish great things in their lives.

Dating can be awkward. You can look stupid and feel

even more stupid. You must continually leave your comfort zone. Add a missing hand to the relationship equation and awkwardness is increased exponentially.

After dinner that night, Dax and Ashley walked around the Southern Utah Campus. Dax strategically began the walk on the right side of Ashley to make sure both their hands could be held. They interlocked fingers and walked for hours and talked about everything. Dax learned an easy way to get past the awkwardness quickly and humorously. They finished their walk in front of Ashley's house. He pulled her in for a good night kiss. The kiss was practically perfect, but Ashley did not want to settle for a near-perfect kiss. She agreed that practice was the only possible solution. Dax knew he had a special girl, a girl who would match his tenacity step for step.

In the morning they met at the soccer field for the next round of the tournament, but this opponent was considerably better than the last. Dax knew the other team was talented, so he wanted to start the game controlling the kick off. The referee did not have a coin for the toss. The teams agreed to Rock, Paper, Scissors for the possession of the ball. Dax instantly volunteered, "I'll do it."

The captain of the other team met Dax and the ref at center field. The captains shook hands in unison and then they played Rock, Paper, Scissors. The opponents' captain held scissors, and Dax held his stub over his left hand. He quickly said, "It's rock!" The other soccer player and the referee looked in bewilderment. No one had the heart to tell Dax his rock didn't count or that he was born a

THE BEST AND MOST BEAUTIFUL THINGS IN THE WORLD CANNOT BE SEEN OR EVEN TOUCHED. THEY MUST BE FELT WITH THE HEART.

Helen Keller

cheater. The referee simply said, "Okay, Freakin' Awesome will kick off."

Dax and Ashley walked up to mid field. He whispered in Ashley's ear to tap the ball just to the left of him. The whistle blew. She sent a quick pass to Dax's left foot. He took one dribble and from half field shot a high, curving shot. Goal!

When Dax was in high school, I moved our family closer into town next to Valerie's parents. We sold our animals, leaving the pigpens empty. The new home still had a garden spot and pastures. One afternoon Dax was weeding a row of corn when he found a wandering baby piglet. The dirty, little, mangy oinker was lost and followed him around. He came to me with the pig not far behind and asked, "Can we keep it?" I told him, "Two pigs live better than one."

Dax learned the meaning of what I said about that baby pig when he married Ashley months after that soccer tournament. Life can be hard and cold, but when two pigs live together they can keep each other warm. When one pig gets up for a drink of water, the second gets up to follow. They keep each other going, and they make life easier for each other.

Ashley has greatly helped her piglet husband, and in return, Dax has helped her. She is a medical student and a pretty darn good one too. But there were times when she did not think she could make it. Dax encouraged her, kept her heart warm, and led her to better water. He knows that Ashley is capable of realizing her dreams.

Chapter 19

New Coach

Dax had one more season of eligible play at the NCAA Division I level, but he still had a redshirt year that he could use. Dax decided to sit out the next season while he courted the captain of the soccer team, Ashley. He still practiced every day with the Thunderbirds but looked for another college to use his last year of eligibility. Redshirting is a common college sports term, usually used in conjunction with incoming freshmen and not eligible seniors. Many thought redshirting a senior year was crazy. Dax thought it was his only option. When your coaches say you need a hand to play, you can't just close your eyes, wish really hard, and magically watch fingers grow.

It was hard for Dax to watch an entire season without a hope of getting off the bench. The previous year he received charity minutes when the team was winning by a large number of points. But all he could do now was watch, miserably cheering and remaining as positive as he could with his coaches. During one regular season game, the team wasn't playing well. Coach Carillo leaned over to Dax, who was sitting on the bench: "You know you'd been in the game right now if you weren't redshirting." The statement was an obvious contradiction from what he had told Dax at the end of the previous year. His frustration was pushed to the max.

Dax started questioning the decision to redshirt. He thought about what his mom had told him in junior college: "You are too good to redshirt." He thought it was the most costly mistake of his career, and prayed long and hard for guidance.

ANCORA IMPARO—"I AM STILL LEARNING."

Michelangelo

Deciding to stay a redshirt, Dax ended his search for a different school. He was going to work even harder so Coach Carillo would play him in the next season.

The conference tournament came at the same time as it always did, but Dax did not travel with the team. He finished out his redshirt season by marrying Ashley in the Logan Utah Temple. The reception was fantastic. They spent the following week on their honeymoon in Jamaica. It was the first time Dax left his basketball worries behind. They relaxed on the white, sunny beach and swam in the bright blue water. "It was ten times better than the Utah snow," he said. Upon his return to Southern Utah University, he learned the basketball team had lost in the first round. Not really surprised by the news, Dax was perplexed when the athletic director called in all the current players on the team as soon as they returned from the tournament. He delivered the news that their coaches would not be returning. Dax thought, "I have one year left. A year is not enough time to convince a new coach he can trust me on the basketball floor."

Dax started a second job at the university fitness center at nights (to stay in shape) while he worked as a janitor in the early morning hours. Now done with his bachelor's, he started working on his master's degree in business administration.

Dax frequently ran across campus to get from job to job. On a particular run, he met the new coach Roger Reid, who had an extensive résumé. He had been the head coach for Brigham Young University and Snow College and had assisted for the Phoenix Suns and coached professionally in China. The chance meeting was awkward, and Dax told him he played for the team last year. Coach Reid politely encouraged Dax, and they both kept going their separate ways. Dax hoped he appreciated his off-season running.

Coach Reid brought with him a new assistant coach— Austin Ainge, the former BYU point guard. Ainge was intrigued by Dax and watched him closely when coaching the guards.

The "new guys," or recruits, came to SUU on their spring visits. Most of them had come from the last college where Coach Reid had coached. The first player Dax met was Geoff. Dax told me, "He's freakin' tough!" Dax had no idea that Geoff was going to be the team's leading scorer, All-Conference, and Newcomer of the Year. Dax played him as hard and as physical as anybody else he had ever played against. Geoff was obviously frustrated with the tremendous defense and frequent fouls that Dax delivered. Despite the bruises and scratches, Geoff never complained about Dax. He respected his hard work.

WALKING ON—AGAIN

The real practice started with a three-mile fitness test. Dax was just glad it wasn't a six-mile run on the sandy beach in California like Yuma soccer had put him through. He finished second place behind another walk-on—Lance. He was a hardworking guy, and walk-ons often stuck together. To Dax's delight, some of the "players" quit, while some of the candidates slowed to a walk. The preseason went back and forth between scrimmaging and conditioning.

> IT IS THE DUTY OF A SAINT OF
> GOD TO GAIN ALL THE INFLU-
> ENCE HE CAN ON THIS EARTH,
> AND TO USE EVERY PARTICLE OF
> THAT INFLUENCE TO DO GOOD.
>
> *Brigham Young*

Dax sized up the new people to learn their weaknesses and tendencies. One kid in particular was extremely right handed. On one occasion Dax waited under the hoop. As the righty came in for a left-handed layup, Dax anticipated him using his dominant hand, so he pushed the ball down just as the other player was bringing it up. Instead of going up with the ball to the hoop, the other player went toward the floor. Fully in control of the ball, he turned and threw it at Dax. This was a new experience for Dax. He had been knocked down, clotheslined, sworn at, punched, and kicked, but he had never seen an opponent so frustrated that he threw the ball at him. They had a quick exchange of words chest to chest. Dax robustly stated, "Welcome to D-I!" No sooner had Geoff gotten between them then Coach Reid walked down from the rafters. He called Dax's name and asked him to come and sit next to him and Coach Ainge. Dax fully expected a reprimand and perhaps being asked to find the exit to the gym.

As a sophomore in high school, Dax learned the definition of irony, and it continues to be a valuable part of his understanding of life. That mismatch between reality and the expected was about to happen again. After Dax sat down, the coaches shocked him with an offer for a full-ride scholarship; however, it was to be the team manager/film coordinator. This meant that he could quit one or even both of his jobs, but a team manager's life was not for Dax. He respectfully declined, even though the scholarship money would have been great to pay for the expensive master's degree. He told Coach Reid, "I just want to play." He then turned to Coach Ainge and apologized for getting chest to chest with his teammate. Coach Ainge replied, "You did everything I would have done."

THE PRICE OF SUCCESS

To make ends meet, Dax had to keep his two jobs and start a paid internship with a local investment company, working all three jobs around his basketball schedule. It was definitely stressful. One day, Dax called me, trying to hold back the tears. He wanted to take the scholarship money and get his school paid for. I told him whatever his decision was, I would be proud of him. Ashley came home from work, and he cried some more. He felt like he was never going to get to play. He desperately felt that the coaches did not believe in him or his abilities, and it was almost impossible to impress them. Ashley encouraged him by saying, "This is what you are supposed to do. You are a basketball player." Ashley kept him going. She helped him every day to accomplish his destiny.

> EXCELLENCE, I CAN REACH FOR; PERFECTION IS GOD'S BUSINESS.
>
> *Michael J. Fox*

Chapter 20

D-I BASKETBALL
SCHOLARSHIP

D ax knew what he was going to do. He remembered a quote from Coach John Wooden: "Never let what you can't do stand in the way of what you can do."[1] At that moment, Dax realized that in all of his reading he had never read of Coach Wooden recruiting a one-handed player on any of his championship teams. So who was Coach Wooden speaking to? What Division I players were letting what they can't do stand in the way of what they can do? Did Coach Wooden really have two-handed players who couldn't perform certain skills?

Dax realized what Coach Wooden must have known. Every player has shortcomings, and each player needs to daily improve, even at the highest levels, and continue to practice to be better. Dax had acquired so many skills to help his team win that letting his shortcoming get in the way was a mistake. Dax decided to stick it out—he had never quit before, and this wasn't a good time to start. Preseason practices concluded with the last three-mile test run, and real practices kicked in. The results were the same—Lance beat him, and they were the only two players who didn't get lapped. Dax's time improved from 20 minutes 39 seconds to 19 minutes 12 seconds. Again, some players walked the run

IN SPITE OF EVERYTHING I
SHALL RISE AGAIN.

Vincent van Gogh

and some more quit.

NCAA basketball season officially begins on the Friday closest to October 15 at 5:00 p.m. It was about 5:30 p.m. when the starting point guard tried to dribble past Dax. Always enticed, Dax swiped at the ball but missed, allowing his thumb to hit the top of his forearm. He heard a loud pop as it bent backwards. Walking over to the coach and holding out his thumb for him to see, he said, "This bone shouldn't be there." Coach Ainge drove him to the head trainer, Rickey, who pulled his big thumb into place and sent Dax for X-rays. Since it was his big thumb and not his little stub thumb, a break would be a sure season-ending injury for Dax. The results turned out great—just torn ligaments and tendons, although the pain didn't let up. The bones were fine, but the black and blue splotches lasted much longer. Today, Dax still cannot hold a church hymnbook for too long without his thumb giving out.

PAINFUL PLAY

Real practices started after this accident. Dax winced with every caught pass that season. He taped up the thumb and made sure the black and blue spots were not visible. The coaches didn't need another excuse to keep him off the floor. He tried so hard to make every catch and to shoot well in spite of the pain. Coach Reid made the players keep track of their free throw percentage and report it in front of the other players. When Dax reported his 20–30 percentage, though, Coach Reid responded with, "Oh, well, it's okay." It wasn't okay for Dax. He stayed late to get ten out of ten. Execution and defense needed to be his way on the court, which would mean fewer turnovers, more assists, higher percentage shots, and better execution of Coach Reid's plays. His playbook had sixty different plays.

DNP

"DNP"—Dax hated seeing those disgusting letters in the newspaper box scores. DNP meant "did not play." When his team played against Utah State, Dax felt he could have won that game guarding Jaycee Carrol, who broke the Utah State scoring record, and yearned for the chance to stop him. The next practice, he reinforced his ideas about his superior defensive stopping abilities. He intensified his defensive game by stepping in front of the starting shooting guard, who was driving with his head down. Dax's mouth met the top of the guard's skull, snapping one of Dax's front teeth into pieces. Some of the pieces went into his upper lip. Dax had emergency surgery that night to remove the pieces, but the next day, with a somewhat toothless smile, he apologized to his coaches for leaving practice early. Coach Reid told him to take a few days off to recuperate, but the team was traveling to Sacramento State University, and Dax wanted to go. Coach allowed him to travel along.

A Chance to Prove Himself

Sac State was Dax's first game and test. Down by four points, he went in to "just run the offense." Dax immediately picked up a loose ball and sprinted for a fast break layup, but to the crowd's pleasure, he was blocked dramatically. Sac State quickly made two points. Panic stricken, Dax got the ball and looked for Geoff, the leading scorer. Geoff made a great back cut on his defender and was wide open for everybody to

> **DEVELOP SUCCESS FROM FAILURES.**
>
> *Dale Carnegie*

see; Dax let loose of the ball too late, and it went to the defender—turnover. Instead of the stat sheet showing an assist to the leading scorer, Dax would be listed in the turn-over column—something no coach wants from a role player. Dax came off the court after only three minutes. Geoff eventually brought the team back and they won by four points. After the game Coach Reid told the players that they had a chance to prove themselves in that game. Dax felt like Coach was talking to him specifically and knew he had blown his last chance to prove himself.

FIGHT AGAINST FRUSTRATION AND FULLERTON

Cal State Fullerton was the next big team test, but not for Dax—another DNP. SUU lost 78 to 63. Cal was faster and more aggressive. Cal played Dax's brand of in-your-face defense. It was so hard to just watch his team be manhandled like that.

The next three games were the same, until they played the University of New Mexico. Coach Reid had decided against taking Dax on this trip until he learned that the Pit was literally Dax's home. Dax had never lost in the Pit before. SUU played much better, and it was tied at halftime. The next half UNM came out with some pressure, and SUU let the game slip away. Coach Reid put him in with two minutes left. The radio announcer gave the crowd a nice history of Dax. This was Dax's first and only loss in the UNM Pit.

After the team got back to the hotel, Dax couldn't sleep, and the next morning he was sick. He threw up in the airport bathroom and had diarrhea to match. Their next game was the following night and Dax hadn't eaten, but it didn't matter. He wasn't going to get more than his two minutes of average playing time. The game went from mediocre to pathetic. They were down by eleven, and Coach Reid was angry. With twelve minutes in the game, Dax went in and helped bring the team back by working to get steals and making assists. Geoff made a shot with four seconds left, which put them ahead until a last second shot gave their opponents the victory. At the end of the game, Coach Reid paid Dax a compliment, "You were working hard the whole game." Finally, a positive!

Ashley and her mom, Carol, met Dax after the game. He looked terrible. They got him to the car, where he collapsed, and took him to the hospital to get an IV for loss of fluids, sickness, and excitement, but all Dax could think about was what Coach Reid had said.

The next game was just like normal—DNP. Dax finally had enough of his team being pushed around. He stood up in the locker room and yelled at the guys to play harder. When the opposing team "pressures you and gets up in your face, do it right back to them." He was so angry that his team was being bullied.

The next game was at BYU. During their pregame practice the night before, he pressured one of his teammates on defense, and he caught an elbow above the eye. He dipped to one knee and popped back up to keep playing, but Coach Reid stopped the play as blood ran down Dax's face and onto the Marriot Center floor. Dax walked to Ricky the trainer and turned again, yelling to his teammate, "You'd better play like that tomorrow!" It was his second opportunity that year to get stitches by the same teammate. They lost the next night by fifteen, and for Dax it was a DNP yet again. But Coach Reid saw how enthusiastic Dax was about defense and for the game in general. He started to give him more crucial minutes, not just charity minutes.

After Christmas break, Coach Reid called Dax into his office and told him that a player was not going to return

> IT'S NOT SO IMPORTANT
> WHO STARTS THE GAME
> BUT WHO FINISHES IT.
>
> *John Wooden*

for the spring semester. He felt Dax was playing well enough to earn a full-ride scholarship for his last semester of college. Dax had finally earned a Division I basketball scholarship, and he could let two of his jobs go. He became the first D-I player with only one hand to earn a full-ride scholarship.

University of Missouri–Kansas City was his breakout game. It was a close game, and UMKC had a tough three-point shooter. Reid wanted Dax on him tight. Dax had some quick steals and a good three-point shot. He played only a few minutes, but they were crucial minutes. They lost, but only by three. After that game, Fox Sports wrote about his performance and he was on the front page of msn.com. "He is an absolute hound on defense," said Jeff Goodman, the sports writer. His minutes were still limited, but Coach Reid and the rest of the world saw how important his time on the floor was becoming to the team.

SOME TROUBLING QUESTIONS

One day, Dax phoned me from Southern Utah and asked me what he should do about some emails he had received from a woman who had given birth to a baby with only one hand. She had several questions, including, "Should I keep the baby?" "Did your parents ever consider suing the doctors?" and "Is there any way to fix my baby's handicap?" Dax had taken calls from several people who had difficult questions about life, but these inquiries were troubling to him. I told him that I'd talk to the lady and had a great conversation where I explained the benefits of raising such a child.

Chapter 21

STARTER

The team's conference record was getting worse and Dax was trying to re-instill some fight in his guys, but Indiana University–Purdue University of Indianapolis did not care and neither did George Hill, the conference MVP, who was later drafted in the first round to the San Antonio Spurs. Coach Reid put Dax in at the end of the game when they were down by twenty. Dax got a quick steal and caused another turnover for a quick four points. Coach Reid was again happy with Dax's hard work.

The next game was against Western Illinois. When they got there, Coach Reid arranged a team lunch before the game with a family that drove four hours from Wisconsin. Dax and Coach Reid sat at the family's table, and a young boy with a hand similar to Dax's was able to see him. They ate and exchanged T-shirts. This boy was so shy and reserved that he reminded Dax of himself when he was starting out in life. Dax tried to joke and give "high ones." Dax could see the parents were concerned, and they quizzed Dax about everything. Dax tried to answer all their questions. He set them at ease by saying, "You're doing a great job."

Later, Coach Reid and Dax were walking slowly in the freezing snow before they got on the team bus when Reid put his arm around Dax and softly revealed, "Dax, you're going to start tonight. Now don't do anything we haven't practiced and just go out there and run the offense and play hard defense." Dax was so excited. How do you put five years of college ball and waiting for your chance into a single moment's response? As calmly as he could he said, "Yes, sir." He was now not only the first one-hander to get a scholarship, but he was also the first one-handed D-I starter.

> **PEOPLE ARE SHOCKED BY HONESTY.**
>
> *Noel Coward*

BECOMING A STARTER

Dax texted Ashley but didn't say a word to any of the guys. He still couldn't believe it was real. Coach Reid announced the starters in the locker room before the game, and Geoff gave Dax a quick low five. He told Dax who he would be guarding as they went to the court. Warming up was so frightening for him. His first layup went right off the glass and sailed over the rim, but he quickly calmed down and focused.

The team struggled at the beginning of the game because Western Illinois had obviously watched film of them when SUU had previously cracked under pressure. Dax made a lob pass to Geoff on the post for a quick two points. After that, his nerves settled, and Dax got in a groove. The player he was guarding quickly shaded him heavily to the left. With two hard dribbles to the right, Dax went around him and made a layup with the foul. Shooting one! After making the free throw, the opposition brought the ball inbounds, and Dax took a charge—their ball again. Things were snowballing. Dax hit two threes, and SUU went into the locker room up by ten at the half. He was doing it, and the T-Birds were winning. His first start was a success.

Dax was so energized and ready to play the second half, but the team came out slow. The other team chopped away the lead. Trying to get something started with the next inbounds play, Dax dove in the passing lane for a steal and came down hard on his shoulder with a loud pop. Dax had felt this pain before. He had separated his shoulder against the same team at the same time as his first year at SUU. He couldn't be out for another six weeks! His season would be over!

Robbed Again by Injury?

Dax slowly got up. Although the pain felt the same, there was one difference: this was his little no-handed arm—not his crucial left arm. Coach Reid pulled him out, and Ricky gave him some ibuprofen. He pleaded for some ice. The trainer looked at Dax, puzzled, and asked, "Ice? You're not going back in?" Dax answered by checking back into the game. It didn't take Coach Reid too long before he saw the pain on his face. He pulled him out again. They lost the game by six points. Dax was ready to play through the pain, but Reid was not going to play Dax until his shoulder was better.

Before the next game, Reid announced the starters while the team doctor came into the training room to look at Dax's shoulder. This was a familiar scene to Dax. The trainer prepared a shot of cortisone with some local anesthetic to numb his shoulder pain and reduce the swelling. It was "instant relief." Playing against UMKC

THE GOD OF VICTORY IS SAID TO BE ONE-HANDED.

Ralph Waldo Emerson

again, SUU got down by eighteen points with the start of the second half. Reid yelled for Dax at the end of the bench, "Can you go?" Dax gave his usual "Yes, sir" and checked in.

SUU clawed their way back. It was the best comeback their fans had seen in a long time. Dax scored fourteen points with three three-pointers. By the end of the game, UMKC had the ball with about twenty seconds left, up by one. The shot clock wound down. The dribbling point guard Dax was guarding set their play in motion with a pass to the wing—a bad pass that sailed out of bounds. A turnover. Coach Reid called a time-out and drew up a play. Geoff would come around the baseline, and Dax would screen his man for the last-second shot. The clock started as SUU's point guard dribbled toward Dax—Geoff came around. He set the screen for Geoff, sending his six-foot-ten defender right to the floor as Geoff sunk the basket. The T-Birds won!

Dax was interviewed on ESPN the next morning. The first athlete at SUU to be interviewed live on ESPN, and he earned the starting spot for the rest of the season.

On to Success

The next game was North Dakota State, who had embarrassed SUU by twenty-five points at their place. After the loss, Coach Reid had told their coach that SUU would definitely beat them when they came to their house. Dax liked that attitude. He remembered thinking that the coach's statement was incredibly bold considering the beating they had just taken, but Dax was determined to make it happen. Dax's assignment was Ben Woodside, an NBA prospect and later conference player of the year. Dax frustrated him all night. He stole the ball from him three times, never let him go right, and made him take horrible shots. SUU won by five points. After the game,

Dax met Danny Ainge (general manager of the Boston Celtics), who came into the locker room, and shook Dax's no hand, and said, "You won the game for your team."

They went on the road and lost to the defending conference champions, Oral Roberts University. Coming back home they played Oakland University of Oakland, Michigan. The T-birds were down after the first half. At the start of the second half, Coach Reid pulled Dax just as the team took the lead. Dax hustled to the bench. Coach Reid stopped what he was doing, got in Dax's face, and said, "You aren't playing hard!" Dax sat down, hurt, but like all good coaches, Coach Reid was trying to get the best out of Dax. He needed Dax's fire and enthusiasm.

Their best shooter had made two threes in a row and pulled the game to within a few points. Coach Reid yelled for Dax to check back into the game, grabbed him aside, and asked, "Can you stop him?" Dax replied, "Yes, sir." Dax stole the ball once on a wing pass, giving them a five-point lead. He knew the ball would once again come back to his man. The point guard's eyes met his player's eyes, and Dax knew they were going to do a handoff. He waited until the right moment, sprinted through the two players, and took the ball. He ran to the other end of the court all alone. He could have taken a layup, but killing time was more important. He dribbled to the corner to let the clock run out.

Oakland eventually fouled, and SUU went to the free throw line to win. Coach Reid pulled Dax over to the sideline and gave him a hug. In the final seconds of the game, the crowd chanted, "Dax!

INGENUITY, PLUS COURAGE, PLUS WORK, EQUALS MIRACLES.

Bob Richards

Dax! Dax!" The dream had been realized. He had accomplished his goal. The experiences that he had worked, fought, and cried through had finally united—everything had come together from the time he was born to this moment. Dax was my hero.

Chapter 22

JUST AS GOOD
AS ANYBODY

The season ended with the first game of the Summit League tournament, the usual mediocre finish that SUU had performed. In the last minute, the team was down by four points when Dax made a steal. Out of time-outs, he attempted a three-point shot and missed. The other team scored again, so Dax took another shot for two and made it, but it was too late. It was tough for him to take. He expected a storybook ending because he felt fate was on his side. He desperately wanted to play in that NCAA tournament. He and his teammates cried in the locker room. It was over.

John Wooden said, "Never believe you are better than anybody else, but remember that you're just as good as everybody else."[1] That is what Dax's life has been about. He has been teaching people that he can be just as good. He is not better, but just as good.

After completing his season, he was invited to Italy to participate in a youth basketball camp. He demonstrated skills, talked to kids, signed autographs, and played against some professional players. He thought he could, for sure, find a coach who wanted him to play. He tried out for an American Basketball Association (ABA) team in Las Vegas.

The recruiter said they were "definitely interested." He took his phone number and escorted him out. They never called.

Dax wondered how he was going to make his life as meaningful as becoming the first one-handed starter for NCAA D-I basketball. Then Dax met a high school freshman from Idaho, who also had one hand. She also played basketball and had watched Dax's games at SUU. He went to watch one of her games and it was "weird." He wondered if he looked like that when he played. Every pass that came to her looked like it was going right through her hands, but she caught them all. She was three of three from the three-point line with a steal. She did make mistakes, but, man, did she play hard. At the end of the game, they talked. She was frustrated with her coach and with the loss, and she wanted Dax to coach her, but she was already doing great. She was the best player on the court because she was giving her best. Dax still gave some advice along with the praise.

> IRONY IS JUST HONESTY WITH THE VOLUME CRANKED UP.
>
> *George Saunders*

Afterward, Dax felt bad for that coach and every coach he ever had. They just didn't know what he had inside. It would be hard for a coach to explain why he was playing Dax to a university president, fans, parents, and friends, especially at the collegiate level when the coach's job is always on the line. Dax confided, "I should have felt more compassion for the chance they were taking on me."

Dax's mother-in-law, Carol, told him, "You need to be around people because they need to learn from you. People can never have too much inspiration." He took her advice to heart. He wanted to coach, and he had helped the coaching staff at SUU with their team summer camp. Davis High

School was the largest team at the camp. Coach Reid had mentioned he was really good friends with their coach, Jay Welk. Dax moved to Salt Lake City, where his wife started medical school at the University of Utah.

Dax's new position with Wells Fargo was right down the road from Davis High School. He went in and looked at the gym. It was smaller than his high school gym. He called the coach and asked to be his assistant, and with a little help from his coaches at SUU, they hired him. His goal now was to eventually coach in college and get to the NCAA Final Four.

Remember that word, *irony*. Well, the one-handed boy who was not supposed to play basketball is now coaching and teaching two-handed boys how to play the game. It's not that easy because some of them really need to work on their skills. Who knows? If they work hard, maybe they can get good enough to play for a good Division I program. Do you want to know what else is ironic? Dax has one difficult thing to teach many of the boys. Try to guess what it is. He can't get them to stop being so one-handed. He's constantly telling them, "You were born with two hands, so use them!"

As I write this story, Dax was interviewed on ESPN after a nationally televised game. It was positive, but the anchor asked Dax, "What is it like to play basketball without a right hand?"

I remembered how Dax, during his early school years, asked me the same kind of question. He asked, "Dad, what is it like to pick up a glass of orange juice with your right hand?"

"It feels a lot like the left hand, only most people are able to feel and touch better with the right hand than the left hand."

My response troubled him. He inquired seriously, "Do you mean that the right hand is better than the left hand?"

I knew that he was taking this as a challenge, and I assured him that one hand is not better than the other. Dax was helping me understand how lucky I was for having two hands. I responded, "No, but most people have a favorite hand."

He dug deeper, "Do you use one hand more than the other?"

"Yes, I use my right hand the most."

He thought for a moment and said, "If I had two hands, I would use them the same. Why would anybody let one hand do more work than the other? What a waste!"

Years later in this interview, he was asked to explain what it is like to play basketball without a right hand. If he honestly answered, he would have to say, "I don't have a clue. It feels very normal." A better question would have been, "What is it like to play basketball with one hand?"

Dax was brilliant though. He changed the subject and talked about what it is like to deal with his coaches' perceptions of him. Dax stayed on the positive and productive side with the interview. This is typical Dax—he doesn't want sympathy. He doesn't want others to feel bad. He doesn't want to feel inadequate and will not do that to others. He dealt with negatives too many times in his childhood, so he tried to lift the level of play in others, and in the interview he lifted the level of conversation. He found ways to make life work better and tried to continually make himself fit in and be necessary to whatever program he was involved in.

When Dax was done with a practice session, he knew that he gave it everything he had and can honestly say, "They need me here because I hustle so hard, I make others better, and I have so much enthusiasm. I make them need me." The coach often left the floor saying, "I can't get rid of this kid. He works too hard. It could start to rub off on the other players." After a few sessions of practice, the coach looked for ways to get more of that enthusiasm on the floor and off the bench. He knew if even one or two more players on his team gained that kind of enthusiasm, he could have a winning combination.

Dax has seen what is really there in life. The following examples show how easily popular opinions and pressure can sway us to see what is not there.

Crowds can be for you one day and determined to see you fail the next. Adults can bow to peer pressure as easily as the young. Every four years we elect presidential candidates that make promises we know they can't keep. Americans love winners, and we vote for those who can win. We vote to make our lives easier, make more money, or give us more from the public pot even though it's impossible. For a politician, telling the truth is political suicide. Telling the truth will not win votes.

Dax helps people see what is real instead of focus on what is not there. "Coach, this is what I have. Please don't judge me by what is not there." I have only admiration for coaches who have boldly chosen to put him on the floor.

> ## MY LIFE IS MY MESSAGE.
>
> *Mahatma Gandhi*

It is not an easy position to be in. The coach may say, "Do I play this handicapped kid and risk my job?" Fans say, "Hey, just put the kid on the floor. You know he's as good as the other players." Fans don't realize what happens if the coach loses. To play Dax, the team must win. If the team loses, the fans will object.

Dax continues to call me regularly and tell me about interesting highlights in his life. Some time ago, a coworker noticed that Dax writes with his left hand and said, "Oh, you're left-handed like me!" Dax had a good laugh because he had no choice about being left-handed. Of course, he loves being left-handed and loves having that left hand, but

> **ENDURE AND KEEP YOUR-SELVES FOR DAYS OF HAPPINESS.**
>
> *Virgil*

he did not choose to be left-handed. It was "handed" to him. It gives him great comfort and peace. But if he didn't have it, he would still find a way to succeed with no hands. Mastering the physical aspects of athletics was a given in Dax's development, but often what is overlooked is the emotional and mental traits that are needed to succeed. Mastering the "stub" dribble was tedious, but along the way Dax picked up several "success" tools.

SUCCESS FACTOR 1—A SENSE OF HUMOR

Always keep your sense of humor. Dax has cultivated a sense of humor since his toddler years. He knows how hard life can get, but he chooses the attitude, "Please don't feel sorry for me." He chooses to be happy and to laugh at life. Whenever Dax entertains or speaks to youth groups and he wants to set them at ease, he will raise his right arm to the square and bend his wrist forward. Then he will bob his forearm back and forth, producing an image of a duck "ducking." It never fails to produce a hearty laugh from young people. Self-effacing humor is where he can laugh at himself. It makes others comfortable around him because he realizes that many people don't know how to approach a "handicap."

When Dax was in my high school English class, I had to regularly allow time for his humor. My lesson plans contained good inoffensive humor. Good humor does not belittle or bully others. Laughing releases brain chemicals, and we feel better. When we laugh we forget our troubles. It was the best year of my teaching career. I continued to make it a part of my teaching. The students were more at ease, and school was not such a drag. In short, try to find humor every day. It's better than studying to be an old grouch.

SUCCESS FACTOR 2—GRATITUDE

Shouldn't somebody who is born handicapped be angry, be negative, and feel cheated? In reality, much of our society fits this profile. Every day, I meet people who are negative and chronic complainers. As Dax has taught me, we all have inadequacies, but we don't have to endlessly whine. Complainers and whiners are everywhere. Some of us have more than our fair share of faults, but we can eliminate most of them. Some faults are just mental, while others are physical and can be difficult to conquer. But what is so refreshing about people like Dax is that although they know their limitations, there is nothing they can't do. We label them "handicapped," while they are just grateful for what they have. They have a unique appreciation for what they *do* have and don't worry about what they *don't* have.

Dax possesses a healthy dose of uncommon gratitude, and I can remember only one time when he was not grateful for what he had. In the third or fourth grade, he came home and asked me why he couldn't be like other boys. I knew what he meant. I told him God made him special so that he could be special.

Dax is grateful for what his mother gave him. He has one of the most coordinated bodies ever and an excellent mind. He never blamed his

IN EVERYONE'S LIFE, AT SOME TIME, OUR INNER FIRE GOES OUT. IT IS THEN BURST INTO FLAME BY AN ENCOUNTER WITH ANOTHER HUMAN BEING. WE SHOULD ALL BE THANKFUL FOR THOSE PEOPLE WHO REKINDLE THE INNER SPIRIT.

Albert Schwietzer

mother or me for what he didn't get. To his delight, he learned that most college and high school basketball players overrate their ambidexterity, and they are quite uncoordinated with one of their hands. In essence, they are just like him.

After Dax was married, he told me how much he likes going to church, games, plays, and concerts because he can hold his wife's hand all through the event. He said that intertwining his fingers with another person's fingers is an amazing sensation, and he is so grateful for that experience. After seeing him grow for twenty-five years, I realized that he had never sat still and intertwined his fingers on his own. How could he? He told me that he is afraid that she will grow tired of his fascination with holding hands because it is so incredible. He's grateful for a good life; a strong and beautiful wife; a good, strong, and coordinated left hand; and a great sense of humor.

SUCCESS FACTOR 3—HUMILITY

As a junior in high school, Dax had thirty-four soccer goals and as a senior he scored forty-six. As a senior he played in the state championship game in Las Cruces, New Mexico. They played a semifinal game late on Friday night against Los Alamos, New Mexico, and his team won in two golden goal overtimes and a shoot-out with eleven kickers shooting penalty kicks. The game lasted for almost three hours. The championship game was scheduled for nine o'clock the following morning, but when the game started Dax's team had no legs. Dax was double- and triple-teamed. He got two yellow cards, which led to a soft red card and removed him from the game. Dax's mom was ready to march onto the field. The game was lost 3–0 but hard fought by mother and son.

After sitting for an hour, I got up and walked down to the concession stand. Two young grade school boys were standing next to the fence, and I could tell that they were talking about Dax. One boy turned to the other and said, "He's really a good basketball player. I saw him play." Not to be outdone, the other boy said, "But he's a better soccer player." The first boy came back with a comment that completely topped the other, "Duuuh, he has two feet!" The contest of words was over.

How could that be challenged? As I walked away, I wondered if the boy had spoken the truth. Was Dax a better player because he had two feet? And even more important, was he a better basketball player because he was born one-handed? Dax challenged these beliefs. Adults and youth often change how they feel, but nobody likes to admit they are wrong. Only strong people say, "I am wrong."

For example, one of Dax's biggest fans was his maternal grandfather, Merwyn Sherwood. He wanted Dax to excel and loved watching whatever sport Dax pursued. When Dax's first baseball season came around, Grandpa Sherwood wanted to present his grandson with his first baseball glove. He wanted it to be a special moment and asked us to come over to their house. We walked down the street to his house, and he asked us to sit down. Nobody knew what he had planned. He went to the back room and brought out a brand new glove. With a gleam in his eye, he handed the glove to Dax and then gave him a hug. Dax hugged him back and stared at the bright and beautiful leather that the glove was made of. It was impressive, oiled, and ready to go. Grandpa Sherwood had taken the glove to the workshop and had prepared it for play.

Dax turned the glove over and over, trying desperately to find a hand to put it on, and then we all realized something. It was a glove that was made for a right hand. Grandpa took the glove back and with a look of sad regret said, "What was I thinking? How could I have made that mistake?" Of course, he had never seen Dax play baseball before, but as he watched Dax manipulate the glove, he realized a left-handed player needs a right-handed glove, but for Dax he needed a glove for his left hand because he threw and caught with the same hand. Grandpa Merwyn lamented through strength of character and admitted, "I was wrong." We all learned from his example.

Success Factor 4—Forgiveness

Ashley once asked Dax, "Aren't you so mad at all the coaches for not playing you? Don't you wish Coach Reid would have played you the whole season?" Dax responded with an immediate no. He responded, "To coach me would be ten times more difficult than a normal player, and I can't help but love Coach Reid. He gave me a chance that no one else ever did."

Dax never would have made it through little league play and especially middle school if he hadn't learned to forgive and do it quickly. Forgiveness does not mean carrying a grudge for the rest of your life. Don't carry grudges—get rid of them. Grudges have great negative power. They push us off track. Grudges can grow into hate, and hate destroys.

Following the Civil War, former confederate General Robert E. Lee visited the beautiful home of a wealthy Kentucky widow. After lunch the widow asked General Lee to accompany her to the porch. From this vantage point she directed General Lee's attention to a once magnificent magnolia tree that Union artillery fire had badly burned. The lady cried while describing the greatness of the tree that provided so many years of beauty and shade. She fully expected General Lee to sympathize with her and take her loss in the same manner. Lee finally admonished, "My dear Madam, cut it down and forget it."[2]

General Lee's words are a great example of avoiding and

destroying grudges before they are allowed to fester into hatred. Don't forget bad experiences, because they help to shape your future, but don't allow them to become obstacles for your entire life.

I have seen many students who carry grudges around for an entire year even though somebody says, "Just kidding." Often, they are not just kidding. Words are weapons for good or bad. Dax has felt the sting of words. At ball games, words were spewed from the stands in order to get him to quit. He ignored them or let them go quickly. Quickly forgiving requires less patience and drains less energy, and you can get on with winning sooner.

In the 1980s, I worked for a power company where management and the union were always bickering and backbiting. It was a stressful working environment. The favorite mode of motivation was threatening employees with discipline or termination. One day as I read a terse memo on a bulletin board, I remembered what my Grandfather Ray Lot Richardson said about a horse named Patches. Patches was a good, steady horse but was not the fastest in the herd. My older cousin approached Grandpa and asked him how to make the horse run faster. My grandfather said, "Now, remember you don't use spurs on a good horse."

I quickly erased the entire message from the board and wrote my grandfather's words on it. Later that day, I heard that the management was upset that someone had erased the directives and had written "something else." Many people had seen my message. The words began to stick in their heads, attitudes started to change, and both sides began to adopt the idea. Good horses don't need spurs, so why are we at each other every day?

Dax has practiced being positive. His quote collection inspired his attitude. Positive messages have the power to change lives. Working three jobs, trying to support a family,

> I'VE BEEN MOTIVATED BY . . .
> OVERCOMING THE HURDLES
> AND OBSTACLES THAT FACE ME.
>
> *Andre Agassi*

slugging it out every day on the dummy squad is discouraging, not devastating. Dax's "insane schedule" at Yuma made me afraid for him, but another trait helped him stay on track.

SUCCESS FACTOR 5—BOLDNESS

No bigger case for boldness could be made than what Steve Scott showed as Dax's high school varsity coach. He understood that putting Dax on the floor was risky and he could lose his job, but he recognized Dax's talents and several of the above qualities. It is one thing to put a one-handed senior on the floor who has spent five years at the college level slugging it out. It is quite another to risk putting a one-handed sophomore on a high school varsity program that hadn't been to the "big dance" in twenty-three years.

Yes, Coach Scott received his fair share of administrators' "ahems." The school principal scheduled him for several gripe session visits with "disgruntled parents of hardworking seniors" after practices. Venom flowed when he lost a game. Parents listed reasons for the loss, and one was usually an allusion to a "charity player." Even bolder was Scott's decision to place a freshman on the varsity team to play beside Dax.

Coach Scott felt it would be worth it at the end of the season. The goal was never out of sight, and turning a program around requires vision. How many coaches have never seen a state championship? His bold plans turned into a three-peat championship affair.

Boldness ensures that we are operating above the fear

level. A "no fear" moment occurred in Dax's junior year in high school. He was competing in four sports to increase his chances for a scholarship. Track and field and the baseball program were concurrent, making it difficult to attend all the meets since baseball was his first choice. On one weekend the baseball and track teams were both competing in Aztec, New Mexico. Several small schools from Colorado attended as well, and the meet was full of competitors. The organizers had a difficult time keeping everything organized and the right runners lined up.

Dax was the first baseman for the baseball team, and he was a high hurdler for the track team. The high hurdles began at 9:00 a.m. Each time his baseball team came into the dugout, they had to listen to the track starter's pistol just behind them. With each pistol shot, he grew more nervous "just sitting in the dugout." Dax's baseball coach was a firm believer in dual sport participation. While Dax was sitting in the dugout between innings, his name was announced to be in lane one for the high hurdles. To the crowd's amazement a baseball player jumped the chain link fence and crouched in the first lane without using the starting blocks. The gun sounded, and the runners took off, attempting to smoothly clear the ten hurdles in 110 meters.

Officials and timers at the finish line had puzzled looks on their faces. The baseball player crossed the line first, and timers and officials began questioning each other. Two ladies with clipboards looked for a baseball player entered on the official roster. Four coaches approached the track referee and complained that the baseball player was not in an official uniform and should be disqualified. Two officials reached into their back pockets for rule books and began thumbing through the pages. They found that the New Mexico rules stated that the runner simply had to be in a "school issued uniform." The baseball uniform was "school issued," so the

> THE LIVES OF GREAT MEN ALL
> REMIND US, WE CAN MAKE OUR
> LIVES SUBLIME; AND LEAVE
> BEHIND US, FOOTPRINTS ON
> THE SANDS OF TIME
>
> *Henry Wadsworth Longfellow*

baseball player's participation, time, and placement were legal.

Dax never knew about the protests. He immediately turned and ran back to the baseball field because he "just wanted to play." It all happened so fast the crowd and officials were questioning who the baseball player was. Dax's run and retreat occurred in less than forty seconds.

SUCCESS FACTOR 6—ENTHUSIASM

The ancient Greeks knew that men were capable of amazing feats of strength—physical and spiritual. Heroes were born among them and on the mountaintops. Something entered into a man and helped him perform beyond his own capabilities. When a man possessed this uncommon characteristic, they believed that a God had entered into that person. They coined a word that meant "a condition of having a God within," or enthusiasm. When Dax was leaving the floor after winning his first state championship, Mike Brown's son was with him. Just as he passed Dax, he turned to his father and said, "That is the kind of player that it takes to win it all." During that game Dax played with tremendous enthusiasm. The Browns knew about enthusiasm because that was how they played in the 1990s.

While Dax sat on the bench for most of his final year at SUU, the team was only winning 22 percent of their games. When the coaches finally decided to put him on the floor in the final games of their season, the team won 75 percent of their games. How was this possible? How could the team improve in such a short time? The answer is the sixth success factor—enthusiasm. Yet this is where motivation drops out and the word *inspiration* comes in. Enthusiasm is contagious.

SUCCESS FACTOR 7—BE RELENTLESS

I received this email from Dax while he was at SUU:

> *Severe diarrhea, dislocated thumb, separated shoulder, bruised ribs and lung, stitches twice by my own teammates, tooth knocked out, just got out of surgery. Not sleeping most nights, heavier pain killers just make me constipated. They don't kill the pain but they help with the diarrhea. I have a bad infected scratch from another player healing slowly. Don't quite know just where my life should go.*

Tenacity and persistence are needed to do things people say can't be done. Often, it was easy to spot when Dax's opposition gave up. His relentless "absolute hound on defense" attitude helped the opposition decide to quit early.

Each of us can make a difference. We can be the difference in others' lives. Obstacles get in our way, and we forget our way. We forget our goals. We must choose each day to reconnect and recommit. Remember, we all have a divine purpose. A hero is in all of us. We can be the hero for so many people, but we have to choose that path. Life works with a sense of humor, gratitude, humility, forgiveness, boldness, enthusiasm, and relentlessness. Life will never be fair. Heroic actions come from committed players. Make the commitment, play the game, and win.[3]

CONCLUSION

My other children and grandchildren will read this book, and I want them to know that I love all of them. I hope that all of their children are born with all ten toes and ten fingers, but if they are someday met by a little stranger who smiles up at them and doesn't have all of the expected parts, consider the following passages that I shared with Dax several years ago. I will never be sorry for the birth of this "wonderful son that can so astonish a mother."[1]

I have allowed his struggles and example to make me a better person. My faith has been strengthened by his life. I like what Rabbi Abraham Heschel said, "Faith like Job's cannot be shaken because it is the result of having been shaken."[2] Our lives have seen considerable "shakes," and as Viktor Frankl said, "A weak faith is weakened by predicaments and catastrophes whereas a strong faith is strengthened by them."[3]

For parents who are questioning a pregnancy from some troubling and suspicious image or medical report, consider the following Biblical passage also. I have seen its fulfillment.

> And his disciples asked him, saying, Master, who
> did sin, this man, or his parents, that he was born blind?

Jesus answered, Neither hath this man sinned, nor his parents: but that the works of God should be made manifest in him. (John 9:2–3)

* * *

The basketball camp Dax went to when he was twelve years old was held at BYU. Later, when Dax was speaking at a girls' basketball camp, someone asked him what he would say to that coach now. Dax replied, "I would probably say thank you."

Afterword

THE TITLE FOR THIS BOOK BEGAN WHEN DAX STARTED TO
play little league basketball in the fourth grade. We were
playing at the Boys and Girls club in Farmington, New
Mexico. I was an assistant coach at the time and noticed
Dax's determination on each play up and down the floor. I
mouthed the word *stubborn* to myself and quickly realized
the negative connotation that it carries. We won the game
and celebrated.

As we traveled home, Valerie and I discussed our son's
attitude on the floor. While she talked, I realized that the
word *stubborn* was a perfect description that competing
players could use to depict Dax. Even more important, I
realized that the two syllables of the word were "stub" and
"born." Indeed, Dax was born with a stub. I went home and
researched the etymology of the word, and indeed, it did
come from the word *stub* or *stump*. How the ending origi-
nated seems to be unclear, but as we know, some words
evolve strangely. I thought, "No doubt, somewhere, years
ago, a child born with a stub impressed its parents with
dogged determination and unyielding qualities. These traits
needed a descriptive label and stub-born came to life."

When Dax turned fourteen years old, he challenged

me to a game of one-on-one. He told me that he was tired
of getting beat and if I beat him that day, it would be my
last win. Usually, I could easily shoot three-pointers and
gain the lead. But not that day. Dax was all over me, and I
could hardly even breathe because he was on me so tightly.
I never beat him again. During my demise and lesson in
being humble, a new word came to my mind for his dogged
persistence—*relentless*. I liked that word much better. It had
no negative side to it.

Relentless became our motto—and it still is—and now
the title.

Notes

PREFACE

1. Dave Thomas, "In His Words," http://www.wendys.com/dave/flash.html.

CHAPTER 7

1. Joyce Brothers, "Quotes," http://www.angelfire.com/nj2/division9/quotes.html.
2. Victor Hugo, "The Importance of Good Thinking," http://www.thevinetoday.com/word/archive/2007/07/29.
3. Shakespeare, "Sweet Are the Uses of Adversity," http://www.enotes.com/shakespeare-quotes/sweet-uses-adversity.
4. Edgar Guest, "Sofine's Joyful Moments," http://www.sofinesjoyfulmoments.com/quotes/you.htm.
5. Shakespeare, "Sweet Are the Uses of Adversity," http://www.enotes.com/shakespeare-quotes/sweet-uses-adversity, accessed

CHAPTER 10

1. Eleanor Roosevelt, "Quotationsbook," http://www.quotationsbook.com/quote/20848/.
2. Martin Luther King, Jr., "American Rhetoric," http://www.americanrhetoric.com/speeches/mlkihaveadream.html.
3. Winston Churchill, "Never Give in," http://www.winstonchurchill.org/learn/speeches/speeches-of-winston

-churchill/103-never-give-in.

4. John Wayne, "Famous Quotes at QuoteDB," http://www
.quotedb.com/quotes/2437.

Chapter 11

1. William Shakespeare, "William Shakespeare Quotes,"
http://www.brainyquote.com/quotes/quotes/w/william
sha101365.html.
2. Casey Stengel, "Casey Stengel Quotes," http://en.thinkexist
.com/quotes/casey_stengel/
3. Victor Hugo, "Will and Willpower," http://quotationsbook
.com/quote/41382/.

Chapter 12

1. Rudyard Kipling, "Rudyard Kipling Poems," http://www
.everypoet.com/archive/poetry/Rudyard_Kipling.

Chapter 13

1. Grantland Rice, "Grantland Rice Quotes," http://www
.brainyquote.com/quotes/authors/g/grantland_rice.html.

Chapter 16

1. Jim Valvano, "Jim Valvano Quotes," http://www.brainyquote
.com/quotes/quotes/j/jimvalvano358454.html.

Chapter 20

1. John Wooden, "Perseverence," http://www.freebase.com/
view/quotationsbook/quote/30079.

Chapter 22

1. John Wooden, "Perseverence," http://www.freebase.com/
view/quotationsbook/quote/30079.
2. Charles Bracelen Flood, *Lee: Last Years* (New York: First
Mariner Books, 1998), 136.
3. Dax's little sister has admirably followed in Dax's footsteps.

She experienced the death of Valerie and her stepmother, Kristi. A few weeks after Kristi died, I turned to Afton, who was seventeen, and asked her what she planned to do with her life. She replied, "I'm going to be a nurse."

We love those we serve. We care about those we care for. Afton had cared for her first and second mothers. The more she served her sick mothers, the more her love for them grew. Afton knows from good examples, such as Dax, that difficulties can strengthen preparation. Stones polish and sharpen steel. Rough-edged rocks become smooth and beautiful by colliding with other rocks. She has become a caring and empathetic person.

CONCLUSION

1. William Shakespeare "Hamlet," http://www.absoluteshakespeare.com/plays/hamlet/a3s2.htm.
2. Abraham Heschel, "Walk It Out," http://www.whoisyoung.com/LifeLessons/Walk%20it%20Out.pdf
3. Viktor E. Frankl, *Man's Search for Meaning*, www.myfavoriteezines.com/ezinedirectory/quotes.

Sources

Agassi, Andre. "Andre Agassi Quotes." http://www.brainyquote .com/quotes/quotes/a/andreagass371461.html

Allison, Dave. "Dave Allison Quotes." http://www.brainyquote .com/quotes/quotes/d/davealliso404591.html.

Bennett, Bo. "Bo Bennett Quotes." http://www.brainyquote.com/ quotes/quotes/b/bobennett167508.html.

Browning, Kurt. "Skating Quotes." http://brainyquote.com/ quotes/keywords/skating.html (accessed May 1,2007)

Bryant, Paul. "Paul Bryant Quotes." http://thinkexist.com/ quotation/if-you-believe-in-yourself-and-have-dedica- tion/347124.html.

Byron. "Lord Byron Quotes." http://www.brainyquote.com/ quotes/quotes/l/lordbyron150381.html.

Carnegie, Dale. "Dale Carnegie." http://www.quotesdaddy.com/ quote/209677/dale-carnegie/develop.

Carrey, Jim. "Desperation Quotations." http://www.brainyquote .com/words/de/desperation153359.html.

de Cervantes, Miguel. "Miguel de Cervantes Quotes." http://www .brainyquote.com/quotes/authors/m/miguel_de_cervantes .html.

Churchill, Winston. "Success Quote View." http://www.schipul
.com/en/q/?2481.

Confucius. "Confucius Quotes." http://www.brainyquote.com
/quotes/quotes/c/confucius161594.html.

Coward, Noel. "Noel Coward Quotes." http://www.saidwhat
.co.uk/quotes/favourite/noel_coward.

Drescher, Fran. "Grief Quotes." http://brainyquote.com/quotes/
keywords/grief.html.

Eastwood, Clint. "Clint Eastwood Quotes." http://www
.brainyquote.com/quotes/quotes/c/clinteastw392797.html.

Edison, Thomas A. "Thomas A. Edison Quotes." http://www
.brainyquote.com/quotes/quotes/t/thomasaed131293.html.

Edwards, Tryon. "Hell Quotes, Proverbs, and Sayings." http://
www.sayingsnquotes.com/quotations-by-subject/hell-quote.

Eliot, Charles William. http://www.famousquotesabout.com/
quote/Be-unselfish-That-is/116086.

Emerson, Ralph Waldo. "Victory." http://en.wikiquote.org/wiki/.

Fox, Michael J. "Motivational and Inspirational Quotes." http://
quotations.about.com/cs/inspirationquotes/a/Excellence2
.html.

Gandhi, Mahatma. "Mahatma Gandhi Quotes." http://think
exist.com/quotation/my_life_is_my_message/214996.html.

van Goethe, Johann Wolfgang. http://www.famousquotes.com/
show/1026328/.

Hart, Louise. "Louise Hart Quotes." http://www.brainyquote.com/
quotes/quotes/l/louisehart402988.html.

Hill, Napoleon. "Napoleon Hill Quotes." http://www.brainyquote
.com/quotes/quotes/n/napoleonhi152870.html.

James, William. "William James Quotes." http://www.quotesand
poem.com/quotes/showquotes/author.

Johnson, Samuel. "Samuel Johnson Quotes." http://www .brainyquote.com/quotes/authors/s/samuel_johnson.html.

Jordan, Michael. "Michael Jordan Quotes." http://www .brainyquote.com/quotes/quotes/m/michaeljor167379.html.

Keller, Helen. "Helen Keller." http://www.brainyquote.com/ quotes/quotes/h/helenkelle120988.html.

Kipling, Rudyard. "Rudyard Kipling Poems." http://www.every poet.com/archive/poetry/Rudyard_Kipling.

Krzyzewski, Mike. "Hinder Quotations." http://brainyquote .com/words/hi/hinder173560.html.

Michelangelo. "Michelangelo Quotes." http://www.brainyquote .com/quotes/authors/m/michelangelo.html.

Nash, Steve. "Motivational and Inspirational Basketball Quotes." http://www.coachlikeapro.com/basketball-quotes.html.

Reeve, Christopher. "Christopher Reeve." http://en.wikiquote.org /wiki/Christopher_Reeve.

Richards, Bob. "Thoughts about Miracles." http://www.picture -thoughts.com/Miracles_thoughts.html.

Rogers, Fred. "Self-Discipline Quotes." http://www.brainyquote .com/quotes/keywords/self-discipline.html.

Saunders, George. "Irony Quotes." http://www.brainyquote.com/ quotes/keywords/irony.html.

Schaef, Anne Wilson. "Anne Wilson Schaef Quotes." http://www .brainyquote.com/quotes/quotes/a/annewilson379585.

Schuller, Robert H. "Robert H. Schuller Quotes." http://www .brainyquote.com/quotes/authors/r/robert_h_schuller.html.

Schwietzer, Albert. "Albert Schweitzer Quotes." http://www .brainyquote.com/quotes/quotes/a/albertschw105225.html.

Shakespeare, William. "Shakespeare at eNotes." http://www
.enotes.com/william-shakespeare.

Sun Tzu. "Classic Quotes." http://www.quotationspage.com/
quote/24267.html.

Unser, Al. "Al Unser Quotes." http://www.brainyquote.com/
quotes/quotes/a/alunser179952.html.

Unser, Bobby. "Bobby Unser Quotes." http://en.thinkexist.com/
quotes/Bobby_Unser/.

Valvano, Jim. "Jim Valvano Quotes." http://www.brainyquote
.com/quotes/quotes/j/jimvalvano358454.html.

Van Gogh, Vincent. "Vincent Van Gogh Quotes." http://www
.brainyquote.com/quotes/quotes/v/vincentvan401701.html.

Virgil. "Aeneid (Virgil)." http://www.quote3.design19.com/index
.php?option=com_content&task=view&id=279&Itemid=51.

Wooden, John. "Basketball Coach Quotes." http://www.basket
ball-plays-and-tips.com/john-wooden-quotes.html.

Young, Brigham. *Journal of Discourses*. 26 vols. London: Latter-
day Saints' Book Depot, 1854-86.

Ziglar, Zig. "Zig Ziglar Quotes." http://www.wow4u.com/zig
-ziglar/index.html.

Left to right: Lance and Dax, the walk-ons without scholarships. Should Dax take the film manager scholarship they offered or keep working three part-time jobs?

Ashley, Southern Utah University women's soccer team captain, would later become Mrs. Dax Crum.

Dax supported and was supported by his teammates.

Dax does the Triple P Stance: Perfect Protection Posture.

Dax always offered support and enthusiasm to his teammates.

In sports, stealing is good. That's when the work begins or when we challenge others to work harder.

Dax takes time to meet some of his one-handed fans.

During his senior year, Dax became a starter, a dream come true.

Dax developed his defensive as well as his offensive skills to become a key player in games.

During time outs, teammates on the bench rise up and take their chairs out onto the floor in order to meet the players coming off the floor. After three years, Dax makes it to an honored seat.

Dax remembered Longfellow's words: "If you would hit the mark, you must aim a little above it; every arrow that flies feels the attraction of earth."

Ironically, many opposing coaches would call Dax a "pure shooter." The reason: an uncoordinated second hand never got in the way.

Playing point guard stretched his skills. The shooting guard position and the fast break were Dax's comfort zone.

Dax slicing between two Oakland players to steal the ball. Dax's hand is taped to hide black and blue splotches his dislocated left thumb bore. (Usually, it was his stub thumb that would break or dislocate.)

The week before, Dax swatted for a steal in practice, which dislocated his thumb. He iced it that night and was back at practice the next day. Each pass and shot was excruciating, but after three years of trying to convince coaches he was "legitimate," one dislocated thumb was not going to stop him.

Danny Ainge, GM of the Boston Celtics, attended the North Dakota game to support his son Austin, who was assisting Coach Reid. While there, he saw a similar steal and told Dax after the game that it was his steal that put the team over the top.

Dax and Geoff Payne give each other a "high five."

Garret Davis

The other team calls time-out to slow the pace. Teammates congratulate Dax on his performance.

Dax's suffocating defensive efforts often provided motivation and leadership for wins.

Dax and Coach Reid won each other's hearts and respect. This moment brought numerous smiles from the fans.

"They should build a monument for [Dax]. He plays the game for all the right reasons." —Roger Reid, head coach SUU Thunderbirds

Garret Davis

At Senior Appreciation Night. Richard, younger sister McKenzie, Dax's wife Ashley, Dax, and senior teammate Tate Sorenson.

Then they praised him soft and low; Called him worthy to be loved; Truest friend and noblest foe.—Tennyson

McKenzie, Dax, Ashley, and Richard. With her own college basketball schedule completed at Eastern Arizona, McKenzie finally got to see her older brother play Division I ball.

Dax and Ashley happily married. Dax's mother, Valerie, often prayed Dax would find a "good girl who would not mind helping him with small tasks" such as securing his left cufflink, cutting his steak in restaurants, or digging a wood sliver out of his hand. Mission accomplished!

(Note: Dislodging a sliver from his hand with his teeth was, in Valerie's words, "not proper.")

Dax and little sister Afton, who follows his example of relentlessness. Afton selflessly cared for both her mothers who died of cancer in 2004 and 2010.

About the Author

Richard D. Crum received his bachelor's degree in language arts from Brigham Young University in 1999 and master's degree in education from the University of Phoenix in 2007. He spent twenty years from 1989 to 2009 coaching track and field, boys basketball, and girls soccer. He currently resides in Mesa, Arizona.